IN THE
GREENE & GREENE
STYLE

PROJECTS AND DETAILS
FOR THE WOODWORKER

Darrell Peart

Linden Publishing

Fresno

In the Greene & Greene Style
Projects and Details for the Woodworker
by Darrell Peart

© Darrell Peart
Cover design: James Goold
Interior design and layout: Maura J. Zimmer

Linden Publishing, Inc.
2006 S. Mary
Fresno, CA 93721
www.lindenpub.com

1-800-345-4447

ISBN: 978-1-610351-80-5

Printed in China

135798642

Library of Congress Cataloging-in-Publication Data on file

Contents

Introduction   v

Chapter 1: The Arched Pull   1

Chapter 2: Large Proud Finger Joints   12

Chapter 3: The Block & Dowel Pull   20

Chapter 4: Rectangular Ebony Plugs and More   31

Chapter 5: More on the Ebony Spline   43

Chapter 6: The Strap Detail   59

Chapter 7: The Waterfall Leg   73

Chapter 8: Speaker Stands   84

Chapter 9: Seattle Mirror Frame   97

Introduction

In my first book, *Greene & Greene: Design Elements for the Workshop*, I introduced my readers to the world of Greene & Greene. As a woodworker, one of my goals was to find out more about the craftsmen behind the Greene's work: Peter and John Hall. In that regard, I am forever grateful to the Hall family—especially to Gary Hall (grandson of Peter Hall)—for opening up their homes and sharing their family history with me. Many of the things they showed me were significant to the history of Greene & Greene and had not been previously seen outside the Hall family. I had the honor of filling in a few small blanks in the history of Greene & Greene.

It was the relationship of the two sets of brothers, the Greenes and the Halls, that I was really interested in. Much of this can only be speculation at this point, but the quality of work speaks loudly that that relationship was something divine. Over the years I have worked at many custom woodworking shops and it's been my experience that when relations between designer/engineer/architect are less than optimal, the final product suffers. On the other hand, when the reverse is true, the work benefits greatly, as it more than did with the collaboration of the Greenes and the Halls.

(left) Detail of bureau, Chapter 3.

The style of Greene & Greene was also of prime importance in my previous book. I covered many of the more basic elements (and how to build them) and discussed their importance to the overall design. But there is more to a design than its individual components. Where did the various influences come from and how were they assimilated into the style at large? I think we can comfortably say that Charles Greene was the primary creative force, but I can't help speculating on what may have been John Hall's contribution. As is evident by his surviving personal work, John had a well-developed sense of design and was known to work closely with Charles. In any event, the creation of a new style inevitably means uniting previously unrelated elements to a work as a unified whole. In the case of Greene & Greene this never ceased for as long as they were actively designing—new ideas and elements were unceasingly being assimilated.

I ended my last book with a plea to my readers to take what I had presented and "strike out on your own." I offered up the interpretative Greene & Greene work of three furniture makers (including myself) as examples. Each of these furniture makers had developed their own perspective and had introduced elements of their own to the style.

I have been studying the work of Greene & Greene for many years now. What stands out the most to me is the incredible level of thought

Detail of chest, Chapter 6.

behind the almost infinite number of details that became a part of the style. A new detail was never simply created, then cut and pasted here and there when needed. Each use of an individual element was given careful consideration before its use and was quite often "tweaked" to fit the given context. Because of this, Greene & Greene was never static—it perpetually renewed itself—it was in essence alive.

Although there is much educational value in exactly replicating the work of Greene & Greene, truly emulating them on the other hand is something different. For every new design the Greenes took a fresh look. They did not discard the old, but did not precisely repeat it either. Every new design had a life of its own, as if it were a new birth and possessed the family DNA. Each new life introduced new traits to the family gene pool.

With this new book I endeavor to emulate Greene & Greene. I want to encourage my readers to introduce their own decorative elements and to make new use of old elements; to keep the style alive.

Most of the details discussed in this new volume are original to the Greene's vocabulary, but I have also included ones that have spawned from my drawing board (computer screen), such as the strap detail and the block and dowel pull. Both of these features have made their way into the greater world of G&G woodworking. Of the two, the strap has an original G&G pedigree, while the block and dowel pull is something I borrowed from the work of James Krenov. I feel it is a great

compliment to my work when they are used in other woodworkers' projects and mistaken as details original to the style.

Style is not the only thing that needs to be kept alive and ever changing—methods of works do as well. How I do things at this moment is the best way I know at this time, but sometimes there are many ways to accomplish the same thing and each has its merits, and the best way is then relative to circumstances or just my mood at the time. For this reason I have included alternate approaches for a couple of things from my previous book.

In my last book, because I took up considerable space in introducing Greene & Greene, I did not have room for any projects. In this book I have included projects of my own Greene & Greene style design. Projects are a good way to practice some of the skills discussed in both books. Projects are also good in that they focus the attention on a specific design and in so doing assist in developing a greater knowledge and understanding of what makes that design work.

Again, I would like to encourage my readers to take as little or as much from what I have to offer as suits their fancy. Staying within well-defined boundaries is where all good creative endeavors start. Being different for the purpose of being different is not what I am promoting. Let the desire to branch out develop naturally. When, and if, the urge to deviate pays you a visit, don't hesitate—go for it!

Chapter 1

The Arched Pull

A good design should, upon first look, present the viewer with a pleasing set of proportions and a strong focal point. With the initial viewing these two elements should be unambiguous. An exceptional design, however, offers discoveries well beyond the first impression. The Greene & Greene arched pull is a prime example of this. But it is much more than just a secondary detail. Don't be fooled by its deceptive simplicity. If there were such a thing as a default Greene & Greene pull, this would be it. This pull, in its many variations, was used on several original Greene & Greene designs.

The arched pull does not shout or draw attention to itself. Its subtleties reveal themselves only to those who look closely. It quietly performs its purpose in a humble but ingenious fashion.

A pull must be deep enough (protrude from the surface) to allow for the hand to easily grasp it. It must also be positioned so that when acted upon it opens the door or drawer in a smooth, non-binding action.

Often times the depth needed translates into "clunky." The arched pull gets around this by starting out shallow at the ends and gently protruding outward in the center, thus providing maximum depth and easy finger access. This invites the user to grasp the pull in the center where the pulling action will naturally offer the least chance of binding.

A more perfect marriage of form and function would be difficult to find. The arched pull presents the world with a sleek form, while providing full uncompromising function.

The arched pull, in its many variations, was used on several original Greene & Greene designs. Built-in Sideboard, David B. Gamble House, 1908–09. Courtesy of the Gamble House. Photo by Tom Moore.

Built in Sideboard, David B. Gamble House, 1908–09.
Courtesy of the Gamble House. Photo by Tom Moore.

Library table in the possession of the Hall family. Courtesy of the Hall family.

The arched pull. Serving Table, William R. Thorsen House, 1909–10. Courtesy of the Gamble House.

The example presented in this exercise is generic in both its overall size and placement of the ebony bars. The Greenes used this pull primarily for drawers, but occasionally for doors as well. When used on a drawer, the pull usually extended to within 2 to 5 inches of each end of the front, and was placed just a little high of center. When used on a door, the pull was usually (but not always) quite short; just three or four inches long. The ebony detailing varied considerably and sometimes was not present at all.

Getting Started

To start, cut a piece of sheet stock (Baltic birch or MDF) to about 10" x 22". From this you will make a layout template used to transfer the arched shape to the pull stock as well as a router table fence to be used for putting the cove on the backside of the pull.

A. Template Layout

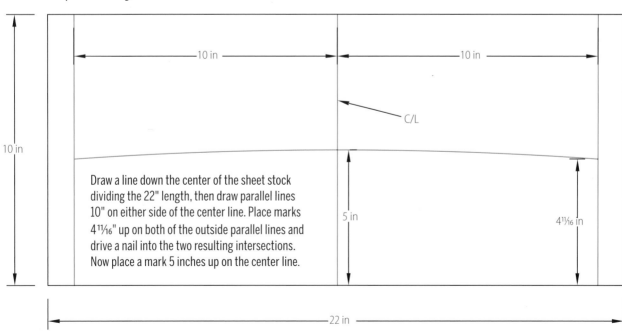

10 in

10 in

10 in

C/L

10 in

5 in

4¹¹⁄₁₆ in

Draw a line down the center of the sheet stock dividing the 22" length, then draw parallel lines 10" on either side of the center line. Place marks 4¹¹⁄₁₆" up on both of the outside parallel lines and drive a nail into the two resulting intersections. Now place a mark 5 inches up on the center line.

22 in

B. Arched Pull Layout

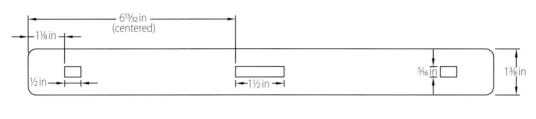

1. Laying out the arch.

2. Even out the mating surfaces.

3. Lay out the location of the ebony bars.

4. Attach a piece of ⅛" material to the scrap wood.

5. For the longer center bar, punch the ends first.

6. Then punch every other spacing as you would with a hollow chisel mortiser.

7. Maintain a firm grip on the punch.

8. Marking the arched shape.

Draw a line down the center of the sheet stock dividing the 22" length, and then draw parallel lines 10" on either side of the centerline. Place marks 4¹¹⁄₁₆" up on both of the outside parallel lines and drive a nail into the two resulting intersections. Now place a mark 5" up on the centerline. These are the reference points for the layout of the arch. Position a thin aluminum bar (or narrow strip of wood) against the nails. Bend the aluminum until it reaches the cross mark on the centerline and trace the results.

The concave side will become a router table fence and the convex side will become the marking template for the pull itself. These parts must mate together well. After band sawing to

the line, attach sticky back 60-grit sandpaper to one of the parts. Run the parts together to even out the mating surfaces. Change the sandpaper to the other part and again run the mating surfaces together. This process should produce two well mated surfaces, but absolute precision is not needed here, as long as the two parts move against one another somewhat evenly and smoothly. When done, set these two pieces aside.

Next, machine the pull to its blank overall dimensions of ⅞" x 1⅜" x 14⁵⁄₁₆". Be sure to make a couple of extra parts for use in later setups. With a pencil, layout the location of the ebony bars. The holes for the bars are produced using Lee Valley square punches (or the chisel from a hollow chisel mortiser). The challenge is to form and maintain a straight line with the smaller square holes made by the tool. To aid in this, clamp a piece of scrap wood of equal thickness alongside the pull stock. Attach a piece of ⅛" material to the scrap wood, lining it up precisely with the back edge of the layout for the bars. To produce the rectangular holes, register the punch firmly against the ⅛" material and use the tool as you normally would (see Chapter 4). For the center bar, which is longer than two widths of the tool, punch the ends first, then every other spacing as you would with a hollow chisel mortiser. Be careful when punching the secondary holes; they do not take a full "bite," and have a tendency to drift unless a firm grip on the registration is maintained.

Now the arched shape can be machined onto the face side of the blank. Mark reference points at both ends at ³⁄₁₆" back from the face. Register the convex piece of sheet stock (cut out earlier) with the reference points and draw the resulting line. Turn the stock over and repeat this on the opposing edge. The idea is to remove just enough material evenly from both sides to form the arch. On a larger pull the ³⁄₁₆" reference point may need to be increased in order to accommodate the full arch.

Use an edge sander to remove the material in excess of the line. For safety, only sand the trailing half of the arch. Turn the pull over, so the other side will now be the trailing half, and use the markings on the opposing edge to sand the other side to the line.

The finger pull can now be routed into the backside of the face. Start with the two short cuts on the ends. Set up a router table with a ⅝" (diameter) core box bit with a zero clearance fence. The height of the cut should be adjusted so as to leave about ⁵⁄₁₆" of material at the top. The depth of cut should be about ¹¹⁄₃₂" (a heavy ⁵⁄₁₆"). Use a block of wood to back the stock up, then run the two ends.

Next, the cove can be continued along the backside of the arched face. Set up the concave half of the sheet stock (cut out earlier) as a fence, about ⁵⁄₁₆" behind the bit so it matches the cove cuts on the end of the pull.

9. Remove the excess material.

10. Routing the cove on the ends, with a backup block and a straight fence.

11. Set the router table up with the concave fence.

12. Keeping your hand well clear of the bit, start the cut with both hands and advance the stock until the featherboard has a secure hold on the work.

13. Continuing the process using push blocks.

14. Mark a ¼" radius on the corners.

15. Remove the excess material.

Add to this set up a featherboard on the out-feed side of the bit. The material will move from left to right. Lower the bit so the operation can be done in two or three incremental passes. Keeping your hand well clear of the bit, start the cut with both hands and advance the stock until the featherboard is engaged. With the stock held firmly by the featherboard, use an L-shaped push block from the rear, aided by a second push block on top to propel the stock past the bit. The final pass should match the cove height on the ends.

To round the four corners of the face, first mark them each with a ¼" radius. Use a disc sander to knock down most of the material in excess of the line. With a sanding block feather the rounded corners to a smooth transition.

16. Feather the rounded corners.

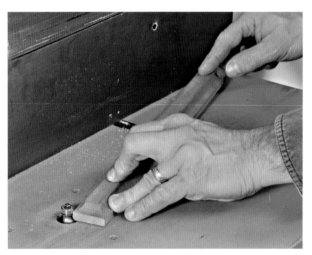

17. Round over all the corners on the faceside of the pull.

18. Clean up the chatter and burn marks.

19. Knock the sharp corner down.

20. Rotate while sanding and blending the face side with the backside.

21. Round-over and blend the backside of the ends.

22. When finished, the backside of the pull should blend smoothly with the front.

With the basic profile of the pull done, it's now time to round over all the exposed, sharp corners.

With a ³⁄₁₆" quarter round bit in a router table, round over all the corners on the face side of the pull. Now, using 80-grit sandpaper with a rubber profile pad, clean up chatter and burn marks left over from machining the cove. To form the round over on the long backside of the face, first knock the sharp corner down with a sanding block. Next, with one hand grasp the pull and quickly move it back and forth making full profile rotations while sanding and blending the face side with the backside. To round over and blend the backside of the ends, grasp the sandpaper and use a flapping motion backed up by your thumb. When finished, the backside of the pull should blend smoothly with the front.

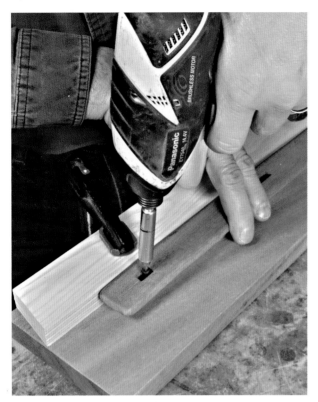

23. Attach the pull to the drawer front.

24. Impart a slight "pillow" shape on the faceside.

Attaching the Pull

The arched pull was typically placed evenly side to side and just a little high of center. Predrill for # 6 wood screws (length depends upon drawer thickness) in each of the three bar holes. Using a piece of scrap to register the desired location, glue and screw the pull to the drawer front.

Ebony Bars

Machine the ebony bar stock in long square lengths about 1⁄64" oversize in width. Using 150-grit sandpaper, impart a slight "pillow" shape on the face side. Ease the edges very slightly, and then sand through the grits until 600 is reached. Buff the face on a buffing wheel with white rouge. Cut each bar to length, about 1⁄64" longer than the individual holes. Slightly ease the just cut edge with 320-grit through 600-grit sandpaper, and then take to the buffing wheel. Slightly back bevel the inserting face, and then spread a little glue around the perimeter of the hole. Tap the bar in place with a plastic headed mallet, leaving the polished face slightly proud of the surface. The pull is finished!

25. Buff the face on a buffing wheel with white rouge.

The arched pull celebrates usefulness and beauty in equal measure. It does not shout above its place in the order of things, but quietly performs both its functional and aesthetic purposes with a touch of genius. It is simple elegance at its finest!

26. Slightly back bevel the inserting face.

27. Tap the bar in place.

28. The pull is finished!

Chapter 2

Large Proud Finger Joints

Proud finger joints are yet another example of how the Greenes took an object of utility and turned it into a thing of beauty. There are a variety of uses for finger joints and each application demands a unique perspective to match the intended use. Visual weight and scale of the piece must be

One of the few known examples of an original Greene & Greene design that used a finger jointed base is the letter case for the Ford House (1908). Courtesy of the Gamble House.

taken into account. If the application is for a major structural component, the fingers would be bold and expressive, as covered in this chapter, while fingers for a drawer, as covered in my last book, would be relatively restrained.

The triple finger joint used as the example here would easily apply to a fireplace surround or the base of a cabinet. One of the few examples of

an original Greene & Greene design employing a finger jointed base is the letter case for the Ford House (1908). This piece was relatively small and meant to sit on top of a table. The fingers were accordingly scaled down to match the overall size of the design.

Our application here involves pieces that are much larger in size than the Ford Letter Case. In scaling the detail up to match the size of the design, I looked elsewhere within the work of Greene & Greene for larger and bolder fingers. The Gamble House entry and stairway offer some very good examples, each nuanced to its specific usage.

Keep in mind the example given here is but a starting point. Depending upon your application you may need to modify your fingers in a number of ways. Use your best judgment together with existing examples to determine what works best for your situation.

Gamble House finger joint as used on the entry stairway. Courtesy of the Gamble House.

Two slight variations of the finger joint as used on the main stairway in the Gamble House (1908). Courtesy of the Gamble House.

1. Back up the cut with fresh material to avoid blow-out.

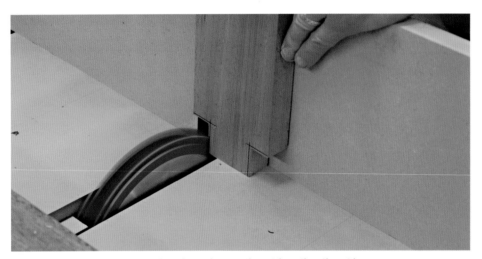

2. First cut one side then flip edge for edge and repeat the cut from the other side.

Mill the Stock

To start with, mill some stock to 1" thick and 3¾" wide. Because the fingers extend proud by ¼" at each end, add ½" to the required overall length of any given project. Be sure to mill out some extra scrap to be used for setups.

Accuracy

My method for cutting the fingers works off the center of the stock. In other words, the stock is machined, then flipped—and referenced off the opposing edge for a subsequent step. As long as some simple guidelines are followed this method works very well and avoids the problems associated with tolerance error buildup.

First of all, the parts must be machined to precisely the same width and be dead on square. The stop used to set the cut must hold its position exactly. If it is bumped and moved even the slightest amount all subsequent cuts will be unacceptable. The cut must be backed up with a fresh material to avoid blowout. And this last one may seem simple, but it is a common cause for woodworking grief. Be sure the stock is accurately registered against the stop. The slightest bit of crud lodged in the way can cause big trouble. Blow out the area around the stop after every cut.

Cutting the Fingers

To start with, set up the widest possible dado in a sled, to a cutting height of 1¼". Clamp fresh back up material to the sled and set a stop to create a ⅞" "notch cut." Make a test cut with scrap material and check the cut for accuracy. If your dado head is good and sharp (unlike mine at this time), you should be able to make the cut without

A. Base Fingers

Layout for round-overs, ebony peg locations, and size of fingers.

"A" = ⅛" radius

"B" = ³⁄₁₆" radius

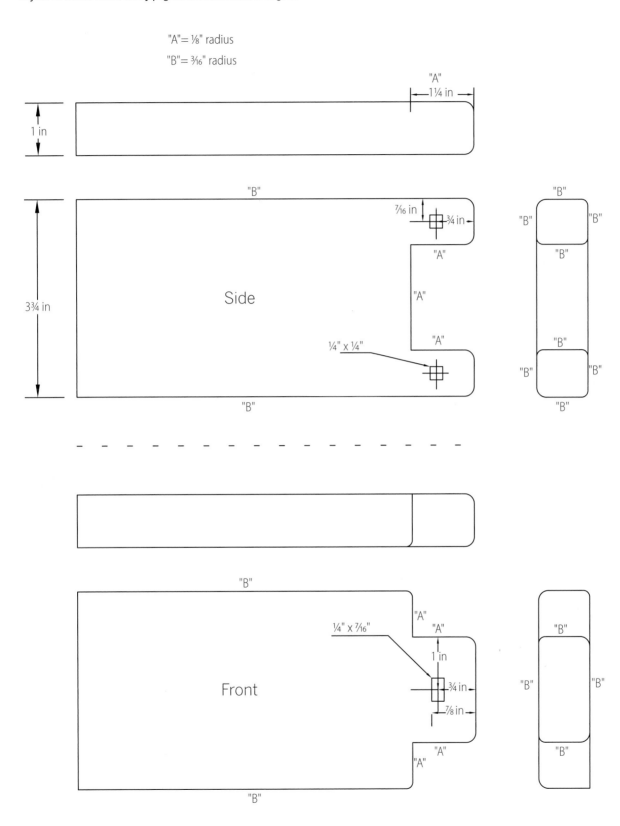

3. Making matching fingers.

4. Lay out the centerlines.

band-sawing away any of the material. If you are having difficulty pushing the material through, go ahead and relieve the cut first. Once a good cut is achieved, run the actual base stock, first cutting on one side then flipping edge for edge and repeating the cut on the other side.

To make the matching fingers, move the stop over so that it makes a cut ⅞" in from the edge. Run some scrap stock making two passes (as before) first referencing off one edge then the

other. There will be a small amount of material left in the center; for now just use a band saw to remove it. Test the cut against the previous cut for fit. Adjust the stop as necessary until the two pieces fit together with only a slight bit of friction. Run the actual base parts, referencing off both sides, then remove the stop and make one final pass to remove the uncut material in the middle.

5. Enlarge the hole incrementally.

6. Measure the hole as you get close to the correct size.

7. Remove the debris.

Cutting the Holes for the Ebony Plugs

It is easier to make ebony plug holes while the fingers still have their square reference. All holes are centered on the width of the individual fingers, but not on their lengths. Lengthwise, the holes are centered on the width of the mating base member. Start by laying out the centerlines as seen in the Base Fingers drawing.

For the ¼ x ⁷⁄₁₆" hole, also pencil in the furthest extents of the rectangular shape. Make the square holes, as described in Chapter 4. For the rectangular holes, first make a normal square hole in the center of the layout. Working out from the center, using both a square, or square saddle, and the existing hole to correctly register the punch. Enlarge the hole incrementally until the extended pencil lines are reached. Be sure to creep up on the pencil lines slowly and start measuring the hole as you get close. Use a dental pick or similar tool to remove the debris left from enlarging the hole. Alternatively, if a quantity of the same size rectangular hole is needed, you may opt to make the punch guide described in Chapter 4.

8. The radiuses for all the edges.

9. Extend the ⅛" radius into the inside corners.

10. Mark a centerline down the face of the finger.

Adding Shape to the Fingers

Refer to the Base Fingers drawing (above) and Photo 8 to apply the appropriate radiuses to all the edges. With a seesaw motion, use a folded piece of 150-grit sandpaper to extend the ⅛" radius into the inside corners where the router bit was unable to reach. Mark a pencil line down the center of the end-grain face of each finger. With a folded piece of 80-grit sandpaper, and again using a seesaw motion, blend the flat face of the finger with the radiused edge. Keep sanding until the pencil line is removed. Continuing with the 80-grit, blend all the edges around the perimeter of the face using a sort of flapping motion backed up

with your thumb. Viewing the fingers from various angles in strong light should identify any facets or lines that need to be blended in. The end result should be a seamless transition from the flat sides to the pillowed face. Once the desired shape is achieved, follow through with the sanding up to 320-grit.

Assembling the Joint

Working first on the two opposing joints along a single side of the base, apply a small amount of glue on the mating surfaces and use a corner clamp or similar squaring device to hold the joint square. Run a single trim head screw (#7 x 1⅝")

11. Using a seesaw motion, blend the flat face of the finger with the radiused edge.

12. Using a flapping motion, blend all the edges around the perimeter.

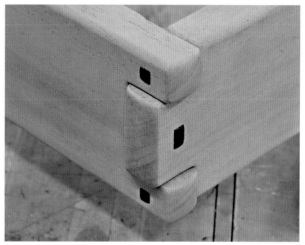

13. Use a single trim head screw.

14. The finished base finger joint.

into the cavity of the center rectangular plug hole. Do not run screws through the smaller two fingers—they tend to split easily. If you do choose to screw the smaller fingers, be sure to pre-drill and be careful not to sink the screw in too deep.

Finish off the base by making and inserting the ebony plugs (see Chapter 4).

Any detail of a design should be used in context. The bold base fingers covered in this chapter are meant to be used specifically with a relatively large piece of furniture. Keep in mind the size and context of your project when choosing to use Greene & Greene style finger joints.

Do not feel the preceding is the final word on the subject. Use what has been laid out as a starting point. If you choose to replicate the fingers exactly as given, that is perfectly fine. If, on the other hand, you have a vision for something a bit different, that is perfectly fine as well. In any event, enjoy the process and let it take you where it will.

Chapter 3

The Block & Dowel Pull

The block and dowel pull is not an original Greene & Greene detail. It is something I unwittingly borrowed from James Krenov's work and added to my design vocabulary. Krenov has been a large secondary influence on my work and his pull is not the only one of his details that I have incorporated into my own designs.

There is good reason to include this non-Greene & Greene detail here. For good or bad, the block and dowel pull has become a part of the woodworking world's G & G vocabulary. It shows up regularly in projects done "in the style of Greene & Greene," and I am often asked about its construction.

In both this book and my previous one, I have encouraged my readers to "branch out on their own." That is, to take from Greene & Greene what you will, and augment to that whatever inspires you. But "mixing and matching" must be done with forethought, lest you end up with Franken-furniture. Merging the block and dowel pull with Greene & Greene is a good exercise in "mixing and matching." I like to think of furniture design in terms of DNA. In this scenario, the building blocks of design are all infused with a common construction thread. When a new element is introduced it can only be synthesized with the material and tools on hand. Every detail appears to have come from the same source. So the

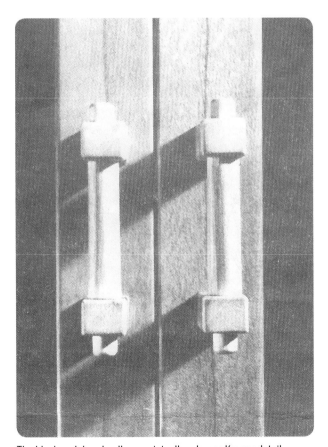

The block and dowel pull was originally a James Krenov detail.

question becomes, if it were Greene & Greene DNA building the Krenov pull, how would it be done and what would it look like?

Krenov, like the Greenes, made most if not all of his pulls in the shop. The block-and-dowel pulls'

The Aurora Chest of Drawers with the block and dowel pull.
Photo by Richard McNamee.

The Freemont Nightstand with ebony blocks (block and dowel pull). Photo by Darrell Peart.

exposed joinery and practical nature is something the DNA of Greene & Greene and Krenov have in common. But there is a key difference as well. The building blocks for a Greene & Greene creation call for the rounding over and softening of all exposed corners and surfaces, much more so than that of Krenov. So, by way of a little "genetic engineering," all the sharp edges of the pull get a healthy softening and round over prior to the Greene & Greene adaptation. Added to this I relied upon my intuition and made the block a bit longer

and more rectangular in shape, than the mostly square, original, Krenov pull.

Like the G & G arched pull, also discussed in this book, or for that matter any design detail, the context will determine the sizing as well as some of the secondary details. The exercise given here is but a starting point and somewhat generic in sizing. I have made this pull in several variations.

To accommodate the wide horizontal drawer front of a lateral file, I increased the dowel size to a hefty ½", made the pull much longer, and added a third center block. In another wide

1. Round-over the end of the dowel.

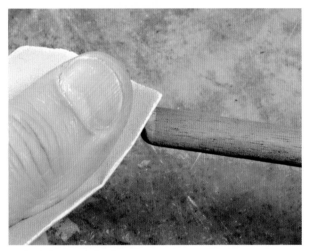

2. Blend the rounded ends.

3. Add a ⅛" radius.

drawer situation, that of a large chest of drawers, I opted instead to go with two standard sized pulls, spaced to line up with the pulls of two smaller upper drawers. The double pulls in this situation also invite the user to use both hands, therefore lessening the chance of binding the wooden runners.

I have on occasion used ebony for the blocks. This can sometimes break up the tedium of an otherwise monotone face and add detail. Be cautious if using ebony as it is very brittle and not happy with some of the machining operations. This will be discussed in detail later.

Another variable is the length of the block and its relative position from the end of the dowel. The 1¼" block length and ½" set back from the end is by no means sacrosanct. They are good default settings, but don't make them sacred.

My first attempts at constructing this pull were not without a couple of minor challenges. Challenges are one of the things that make woodworking fun though. If it were too easy it would cease to hold our interest.

Getting Started—The Doweled Rod

To start with, familiarize yourself with the drawing of the pull (drawing A), then cut a ⅜" dowel to a length of 6". To round over the end of the dowel, set up a router table with a ⅛" round over bit. Line up the middle of the dowel rod with the middle of the bit's bearing and clamp a piece of thin sheet stock (¼" or less) in place to save the registration. To perform the operation, place the dowel against the registration piece with the end in contact with the bearing, and then use your fingers to rotate the dowel one full revolution. Blend the rounded ends of the dowel with 220-grit sandpaper using a "flapping" motion backed up by your thumb. Finish sanding the rest of the rod to 220-grit, then set the finished dowel part aside for now.

The Blocks

Next, mill some ⅝" x ¹³⁄₁₆" material for the pull blocks in a long length, say 6" or more. Using a router table, put an ⅛" radius on the two corners of one of the narrow faces. Next cut three or four (one or two extra for setups) lengths off the stock at 1 ¼" long. These will be the blocks for the pull. As per the drawing, layout the center lines for the dowel hole on the ends of the blocks. Set the blocks aside for now.

Making the Boring Fixture

Boring a hole for the dowel in such a small piece, such as the block, can be a little awkward. There is not much material left on the face side of the block after boring, so it is vital that registration be both secure and accurate.

The fixture illustrated in drawing B and photo 5 not only registers the stock precisely and holds it fast, but also allows for a replaceable piece that backs up the bit and prevents clogging and blowout.

Start by cutting out a piece of ¾" sheet stock to about 8" x 18", then two hardwood blocks at 1¾" x 2" x 6". Referring to drawing B again, with glue, and screws from the bottom side, attach the two blocks in a "T" shaped arrangement. Next attach the two "reference blocks" (about ¾" x 1½" x 2¾") using one of the pull blocks to space the opening at ⅝". Be sure to leave a ¼" gap above the sheet stock. Next, cut out a few strips of ¼" thick material, to back up the drilling operation. The width and length of the backup material is unimportant, its only requirement being to fit in the gap between the reference blocks and the sheet stock. With a pull block placed in the gap between the reference blocks, attach a De-Sta-Co type horizontal clamp to the sheet stock, so when engaged it locks the block securely in place.

4. Lay out the center lines.

5. The boring fixture.

A. The Block & Dowel Pull

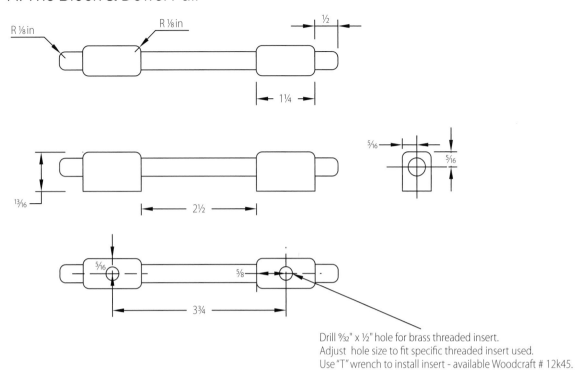

R ⅛ in   R ⅛ in   ½   1¼

13⁄16   2½   5⁄16   5⁄16

5⁄16   5⁄8   3¾

Drill 9⁄32" x ½" hole for brass threaded insert.
Adjust hole size to fit specific threaded insert used.
Use "T" wrench to install insert - available Woodcraft # 12k45.

B. Boring Fixture for Drilling the Blocks

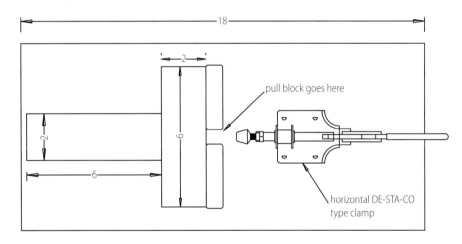

18

2

2

6

6

pull block goes here

horizontal DE-STA-CO
type clamp

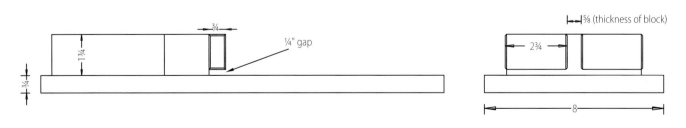

¾   ¼" gap   ⅝ (thickness of block)

1¾   2¾

¾   8

Boring the Hole

Before boring the hole you must determine the bit size. Ideally, the hole in the block should be just slightly larger than the dowel (.007 or so)—just enough so it moves in and out easily with very little friction. If the dowel were exactly ⅜" (.375), making the hole ¼₄" (.015625) oversize would produce a fit that is much too loose. It is common, however, for commercial dowels to have shrunk a few thousands of an inch; just enough for an acceptable fit using a ⅜" bit. But dowels can swell as well, so there are a couple of scenarios you must be prepared for. It is experience in the end that will be your best judge as to which approach is best.

If the fit is too tight, the glue will seize up before the blocks can be correctly placed. If too loose, the glue will not grab. For a slightly looser fit, you can apply a very liberal coat of glue and let it "thicken" up for 10 or 15 minutes before assembly. For too tight of a fit you can evenly sand the dowel by hand to slightly downsize it. For the worst case scenario, use a drill press to sand the dowel down to size. Wrap protective tape around the end going in to the chuck. Sand the exposed portion, then reverse the dowel, wrap the other end, and sand again.

Once the bit size is determined, secure the block in the boring fixture with the rounded corners facing in and a piece of ¼" material underneath for back up. Position and clamp the fixture under the bit so the centerline on the block registers with the center point of the bit. Now bore the hole. After drilling, remove the ¼" material and blow the area out, then reposition the backup piece for the next hole. If the hole was off center, re-adjust and bore again with a fresh block.

Shaping the Block

The end faces of the blocks are too small to round-over using a router table and must be done by hand. The bottom edge that joins with the drawer or door does not get rounded over. With the block in your hand and the sandpaper stationary, put a light bevel on the three corners of each end face. Blend the bevel to match the

6. Position and clamp the fixture under the bit.

7. Put a light bevel on the three corners of each end face.

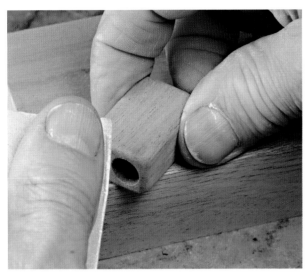

8. Blend the bevel to match the ⅛" radius.

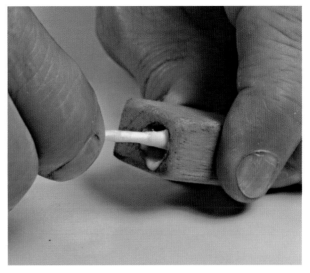

9. Apply glue to the interior of the hole in the block.

10. Slide the first block onto the dowel.

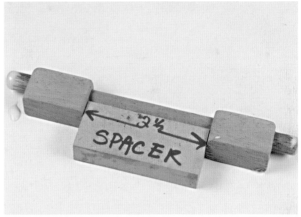

11. Place the second block on the dowel.

⅛" radius round over of the two face edges with a flapping motion backed up with your thumb. Finish sanding to 220-grit.

Glue up

First, make a spacer ½" thick (distance block is from end of dowel) x 2½" long (distance between the blocks) for positioning the blocks on the dowel. The glue up is very messy, so lay down a sheet of wax paper to protect your bench from water and glue. Also gather up two small tubs of water, two toothbrushes, a clean up rag, and some Q-Tips.

Using a Q-Tip, start by applying a generous amount of glue to the interior of the hole in the block. Depending upon the fit, you may or may not need to let the glue sit and thicken for a while. Again, experience is the best gauge of this. If you

anticipate the glue seizing up, you may need to perform the following steps quickly.

Slide the first block onto the dowel using the ½" spacer to register its location in from the end. Next, place the second block on the dowel, using the 2½" spacer to verify the correct distance from the first block. If everything went as planned the outside margin on both blocks should be ½". If need be and if possible (the first block may be frozen at this point), adjust the blocks so the outside margins are visually the same, with the center being maintained at 2½". Before setting the pull aside to dry, make sure the bottom faces of the blocks rest evenly on a flat surface. They do not have to be perfectly flat at this point, but get them as close as you can.

Using a toothbrush, thoroughly remove all the excess glue. Restrict the initial cleanup to the

12. Place the blocks on a flat surface.

13. Add pencil marks to the blocks.

same brush and the same tub of water. Follow up with a clean brush from clean water to remove any unseen residue.

Let the glue set up for about an hour, possibly longer if the fit was loose. Next, thoroughly cover the bottom surfaces of the blocks with pencil marks. Place a piece of sticky back 80-grit sandpaper on a flat machined surface, then run the bottom face of the blocks over the sandpaper until all the pencil marks are removed and both blocks are in the same plane.

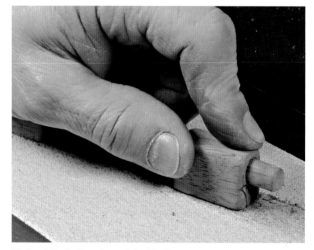

14. Sand the bottom face of the blocks.

Mounting the Pull

The pull is mounted using threaded inserts set into the blocks. The relative position of the inserts must be precisely transferred to the drawer or door. Measuring each drilling location is both slow and a potential recipe for woe. To make this step simple and easy, first make a spacer 3¾" long. This is the exact spacing between the centers

15. Find the center of the blocks.

16. Bore the first hole about ½" deep with the spacer in place.

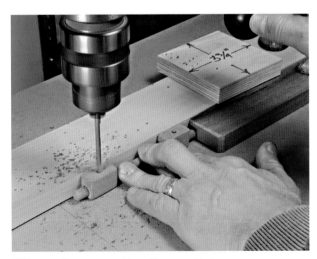

17. Remove the spacer and bore the second hole.

of the threaded inserts. Draw lines representing the exact centers on the backside of the blocks. Drawing the center on the second block is not necessary but may be done for the purpose of verification. Set the drill press up with the correct size brad point bit for the specific threaded insert being used (see page 30). If using ebony blocks experiment with a larger bit until the wood does not split. With the 3¾" spacer between the stop and the nearest block, line up the center lines with the center of the bit and bore the hole about ½" deep. Remove the spacer and slide the pull down to meet the stop and bore the second hole. If everything worked out correctly the second hole should have fallen near the center of the second block. The important thing is to maintain an exact 3¾" spacing.

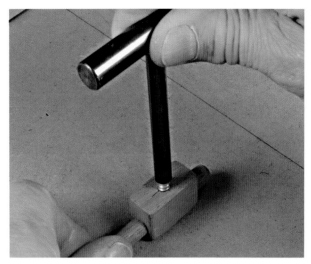

18. Use a "T" wrench to install the inserts.

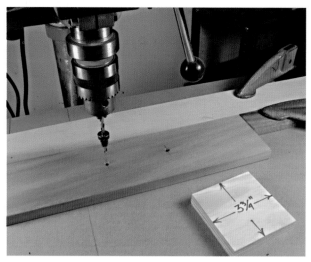

19. Drill the corresponding holes into a door or drawer front using the same 3 ¾" spacer.

20. The finished block and dowel pull.

The threaded inserts I used to illustrate here were originally found at woodworkingparts.com, but have been discontinued. A good alternate can be found at Highland Hardware, sold as item #175311 (8-32 thread). In any event, there are many inserts that will work fine for our application here. Adapt the drilling size and depth to suit the actual insert you use.

To install the inserts, use a "T-wrench," like the one available at Woodcraft stores (item number 12k45). To drill the corresponding holes into a door or drawer front, use the same spacer but change the bit to bore for a 8-32 flat head brass screw with a countersink. As before, draw center lines representing the first hole and bore

(back side up for the countersink) with the same spacer in place. Remove the spacer and drill the second hole.

Give the pull a light final sanding prior to mounting it with 8-32 brass flat head screws. If the spacer was used properly the holes should line up flawlessly. Final finishing should be done with the pulls unattached.

The block and dowel pull can be used for many different applications and not just for Greene & Greene, Arts & Crafts, or Krenov projects. The pull presented here is generic in size and application. Feel free to adapt it to whatever uses you may find.

Chapter 4

Rectangular Ebony Plugs and More

In my last book, *Greene & Greene: Design Elements for the Workshop*, I had a lot to say about ebony plugs—but only square plugs. In the world of Greene & Greene, plugs do not stop at square.

There are other shapes as well, with the most common of these being rectangles. I will cover not only rectangles in this new chapter, but also method refinements and a new tool that relates back to the discussion in my first book. In fairness to my new readers, I will include necessary material from my previous book. But in fairness to my previous readers, I will restate the material as briefly as possible.

The most notable update is the square punches produced by Lee Valley for making the square holes. For purposes of full disclosure; I invented the square punches and get royalties from their sale. There is an alternative method, which was discussed in my last book and involves the use of the hollow chisel from a hollow chisel mortiser. The square punches, however, were designed for this specific purpose and I feel they do their job better than any other method.

On a large project, such as a dining set, there can be hundreds of ebony pegs to make. This

The Square Punch produced by Lee Valley.

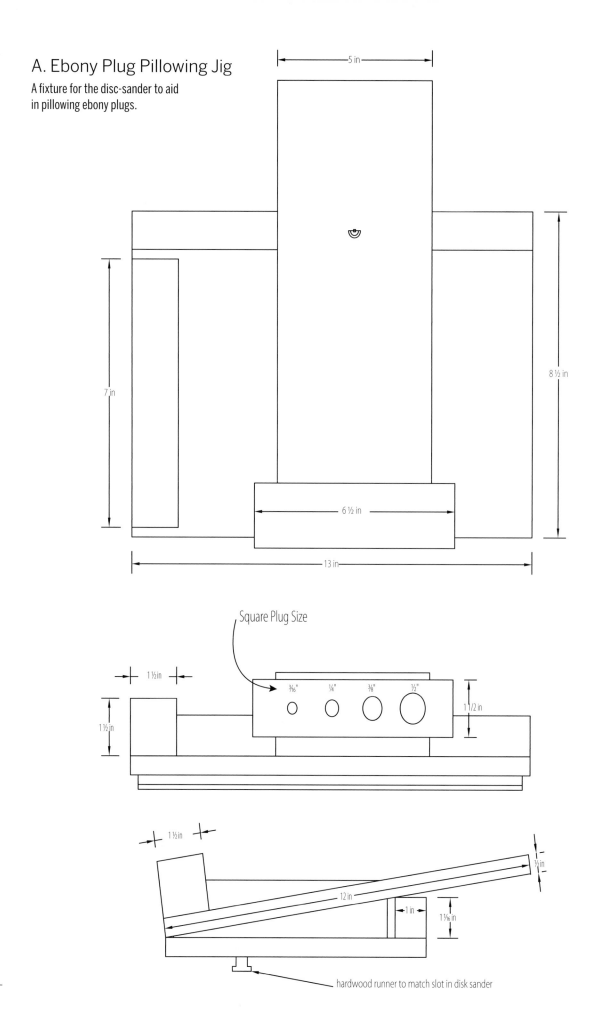

A. Ebony Plug Pillowing Jig

A fixture for the disc-sander to aid in pillowing ebony plugs.

5 in

8 ½ in

7 in

6 ½ in

13 in

Square Plug Size

1 ½ in

1 ½ in

³⁄₁₆"   ¼"   ⅜"   ½"

1 1/2 in

1 ½ in

½ in

12 in

1 in

1 ³⁄₁₆ in

hardwood runner to match slot in disk sander

1. Long rods of ebony stock.

2. Position one finger at the opening.

can add up to considerable time. Efficiency then becomes important, but with practice, anyone can achieve a relatively high rate of productivity. Having spent many years in custom shops where productivity meant job survival, I am always on the lookout for a better labor-saving way, so my methods are never frozen in time. As of this writing, I can produce 99 plugs in a one-hour period. This is with the rods already made, but includes sanding and forming the pillow shape, buffing, cutting to length, and back beveling.

The description below is fine-tuned for making large quantities. If this is not needed, the same basic procedures hold true for smaller runs. Also, the size of the plug will determine the sandpaper grits needed for the pillow/sanding process. The most common sized plug is ¼", which I have used for the purpose of our exercise here. For plugs ⅜"–½", you may want to start the sanding process with 150-grit. For even larger plugs you may want to start with something even coarser.

Whole size chart for pillowing fixture.

Square Plug Size	³⁄₁₆"	¼"	⅜"	½"
Ebony Rod Size	¹³⁄₆₄"	¹⁷⁄₆₄"	²⁵⁄₆₄"	³³⁄₆₄"
Jig Hole Size (dia.)	⁵⁄₁₆"	⁷⁄₁₆"	⅝"	¹³⁄₁₆"

For those who would rather dispense with the tedium of making plugs altogether, there is a solution for you as well: just wait for your kids or grandkids to say the magic words, "Is there anything I can do to earn some money?"

Making the Ebony Plugs

Start by milling ebony stock in long rods to about ten-thousands (light ¹⁄₆₄") over the given size. Because ebony is very hard and mahogany much softer, the ebony will force its oversize shape onto the mahogany, producing a very crisp perimeter around the plug. For aid in producing the pillowed effect, first construct the disc sander jig shown in drawing (drawing A, drawing B). The idea behind the jig is to create a very slight crown, with all four shoulders relatively in the same plane. Many other methods tend to draw the corners down, exaggerating the pillow effect.

Start by inserting the rod into its appropriate hole in the jig. When held correctly, the rod should move freely and rest on only two points, the leading top edge of the hole and the trailing bottom edge. Now turn the disc-sander on and start twirling the rod between your fingers. While the rod is twirling, move it forward until it makes contact with the disc. Try to maintain the rod's position without letting it creep forward. I often position one finger at the entrance using upward

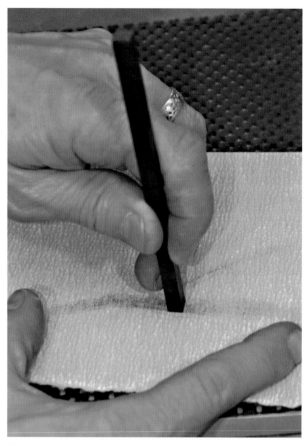

3. Use a pendulum motion to sand away scratches and facets.

4. Finish off by buffing the end.

5. The polished end should have a very soft pillow to it.

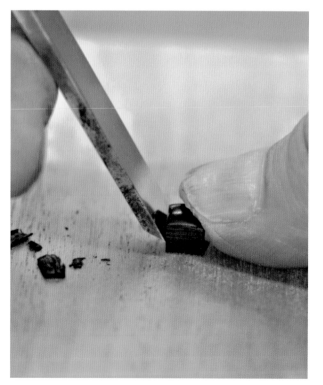

6. Cut the finished plug and back bevel the insertion end.

7. Proper alignment is very important.

8. The points of the punch should now lightly hold it in place.

pressure to restrain forward advancement. It may take practice to produce the desired results. Next, procure a soft pad—old mouse pads work well—and place it under a piece of 220-grit (coarser grits for plugs larger than ⁵⁄₁₆") sandpaper. With a swinging pendulum motion and even strokes, sand away the facets and scratches produced by the disc sander. After three or four passes, turn the rod 90-degrees. Repeat this process until the face of the stock is very smooth and even. Using the same pendulum motion, progress through the grits until 600-grit is reached (220, 320, 600). In my first book I used a "swirling" motion for this part of the process, which tended to draw the corners down excessively. The pendulum motion is a refinement and does not do this.

Finish off by buffing the end with white jeweler's rouge on either a grinder or drill press. The polished end should have a nice warm glow and a very soft pillow to it. Cut the finished plug

end off to about ¼" to ⁵⁄₁₆" long and, using a chisel, back bevel the insertion end.

If you only have a very few plugs to make, it may not make sense to build the disc sander jig, unless future use is likely. As an alternative, the pillowing effect can be achieved by using the above described pendulum motion on the soft padded sandpaper. Just start the process at a lower grit.

Making the Holes for the Ebony Plugs

The holes are very easy to produce using the Lee Valley square hole punch. To use the punch, draw centerlines representing the designated location.

Use a small square saddle (or simply a small square) to insure proper alignment, and then tap on the tool just enough to register the points and make it stay put. The points of the punch should now lightly hold it in place.

9. Drill out the hole to a depth of about ⅜".

10. Punch the tool to the full depth of the hole.

11. Stop to wiggle the tool slightly.

12. The square hole should be exactly to size.

13. Carefully seat the plug.

14. The finished plug in place.

Next, use a regular twist bit that is ⁵⁄₆₄" under the size of the punch, to drill out the hole to a depth of ³⁄₈". Do not use a brad point bit as the spurs will likely incur damaged when they pass through the smaller chisel end of the tool.

Now remove the drill and punch to the full depth of the hole with a steel hammer. Between hammer blows, stop to wiggle the punch slightly as this will aid in easy tool removal. Additionally, treating the tool end with a lubricant such as dri-cote will further assist in this regard.

Before removing the tool from the wood, re-insert the drill for a second time to remove the debris left over by the punch. As the punch is pulled out make an effort to minimize its side to side movement. The resulting square hole should be exactly to size, with crisp, well-defined edges and free of internal debris.

Inserting the Plugs

For the purpose of illustration, the plug here was inserted into a demo piece. Normally plugs are introduced at the very last step in the project, just before applying the finish. If done before this point, clamps can push them in further (an excuse to hone your foul language skills) and final sanding and repair around them is difficult.

Inserting an ebony plug requires a bit of practice and care. It is very easy to tap just a little too much and send the shoulder of the plug in past the perimeter of the hole. Ideally the shoulder should stop just a few thousands shy of the hole. It is better to err on the side of leaving the plug just a bit too high. Use a plastic headed mallet to carefully seat the plug. The amount and angle of the back bevel, along with the size of the plug in relation to the hole, all play a part in how easy the plug taps in. The equation also changes (because of the differences in hardness) when

Rectangular ebony plugs on the Thorsen Server. William R. Thorsen House, 1909-10. Courtesy of the Gamble House.

woods other than mahogany and ebony are used. Practice, as always, is the best judge in dealing with these variables.

If you have tapped the plug too far in, or for some other reason the plug needs to be removed, it is not difficult to do. First, use a center punch to establish a positive starting point for a brad point bit. With a bit much smaller than the hole, drill out the center of the plug. Next use a very small chisel to chip away from the drilled hole until a larger chisel can be used to finish it off. The last bit of plug should just cleanly fall away from the walls of the hole, no matter how long the plug has been in place.

Rectangular Ebony Plugs

Although rectangular ebony plugs are not as common as the square ones in Greene & Greene designs, they are by no means uncommon either. They can be found in a variety of situations. There are no hard and fast rules concerning their use. That is not to say they were used indiscriminately though. A careful study of their placement by the Greenes will bear this out. As a thought-provoking exercise, try imagining square plugs in the place of rectangles on an original piece of G&G furniture. While you may or may not comprehend the merit of their use and placement on an intellectual level, I would venture to say your gut knows the difference and prefers the Greene's choice of rectangles in that specific instance.

15. Cut the stock out in long rods.

16. Use the disc sanding jig if possible.

Sometimes, with a little thought, there is a reason behind a rectangular plug. To the non-woodworker, the fact that the outermost plug on almost every G&G breadboard is rectangular, probably seems like nothing more than an interesting design feature. To the woodworker, however, there is a practical purpose behind this. With the middle section of the bread board glued in place, the top moves from the center out. The outermost edge of the top on each side is where wood movement will be at its most extreme. This is where the rectangular plug covers a horizontal slot that allows the screw behind the plug to move with the changes in humidity.

A close look at my "triple finger base joint" provides us with a definable visual reason for a rectangular plug as opposed to a square plug.

Looking at the joint through the lens of my "DNA" analogy (see Chapter 2, photo 14), we see that the two outer fingers are both smaller and pinned by square ebony plugs. The center finger is identical to the outside fingers, except for being larger in the vertical dimension. It makes sense then that the DNA would call for any secondary details relating to the center finger to also be enlarged in the vertical dimension, thus producing a rectangular center plug.

Making Rectangular Plugs

Making rectangular plugs is much the same as making the square ones. Cut the stock out in long rods just as you would for square plugs. Unless there is a large quantity involved, I do not make specifically sized holes for rectangles in the disc sander jig. Often times, one of the existing holes will work, even if it's a little looser than normal.

The disc sander produces an ever so slight crown, so make sure, if you skip the disc sander and do them by hand, that you start with a coarser grit and a rod that has a good square/flat end. Go through the grits using the pendulum motion to pillow the face, and then finish the process as before with polishing, cutting to length, and back beveling.

Making the Rectangular Hole

With the rectangular rod sized to within a few thousands of an inch and a correspondingly sized punch not available, the question becomes how to precisely and repeatedly size the hole. The solution is to fashion a punch guide from ¼" material. The guide consists of a notch just a few thousands under the size of the plug's long dimension. If possible, size the guide so it self-registers on the stock being worked. Using the rectangular plug found on the triple finger joint (previously discussed) as an example, the notch would be machined dead center and about ¼" deep. The guide would match exactly the width of the stock being machined.

It is relatively easy to machine a notch precisely in the center of the guide. Using a rip blade with flat bottom teeth and a table saw sled, cut first one side, flip side for side and cut again, remove the stop, and waste out the material left in the middle.

17. The disc sander produces a slight crown.

18. The finished rectangular plug, ready to install.

19. Constructing the guide.

20. Draw a line that represents the back edge of the hole.

21. Align the guide.

To register the guide, instead of using centerlines, as you would when laying out a square plug's location, draw a line that represents the back edge of the hole. The guide is aligned flush with the width of the stock and the bottom of the notch is registered on the line representing the back edge of the hole.

If it is not possible to utilize the shape of the guide for registration, then use a square to correctly align the guide.

22. Register the punch in one of the opposing corners of the notch.

23. The inserted plug.

With the guide clamped in place, register the punch in one of the opposing corners of the notch and proceed as you would normally to produce a square hole. Next move the punch to the other corner and repeat the process. A word of caution at this point: Sometimes if the punch is not taking a full bite in the second hole, there is a tendency for it to drift inward. In this case, make sure the two grabbing points of the punch are securely registered before drilling. If the hole is more than twice as large as the punch, just slide the tool down and punch the remaining material. If it's a very long hole and a lot of material remains, punch every other spacing, then go back and get the remaining spaces.

If everything went as planned the hole should be just a few thousands smaller than the plug. You can now tap the plug into place as you normally would with a plastic headed mallet.

This is not the final word on ebony plugs. However this does cover the subject up to my current knowledge base, and I hope it has added something of use to your woodworking bag of tricks. Consider this as a point along the way. Add to it or subtract from it, to get what is of use to you.

Chapter 5

More on the Ebony Spline

Woodworking is not a static affair. If it were, we would never enjoy new innovations or designs. Methods of work should not be immovable objects, but rather considered only the best way we know how at this time. In my last book, I presented the reader with a method for making Greene & Greene ebony splines. While that original technique is still valid, I have developed a new method, which requires more initial outlay in resources, but the process then becomes more streamlined and the results more pleasing.

I cannot claim ownership of the new idea though. That goes to my friend Graham Jackson, who at one time worked for me. Although a brilliant proposal, it had some bugs. The jigs evolved over the period of three or four years with my students and visitors to the shop pitching in with some cerebral heavy lifting along the way. I will not say this is the only, or the best way, to produce the ebony spline detail. I will say, though, that this is the best way I know how at this time.

The ebony spline detail as seen on the Thorsen house sideboard 1909-10. Courtesy of the Gamble House.

A. Template Plate

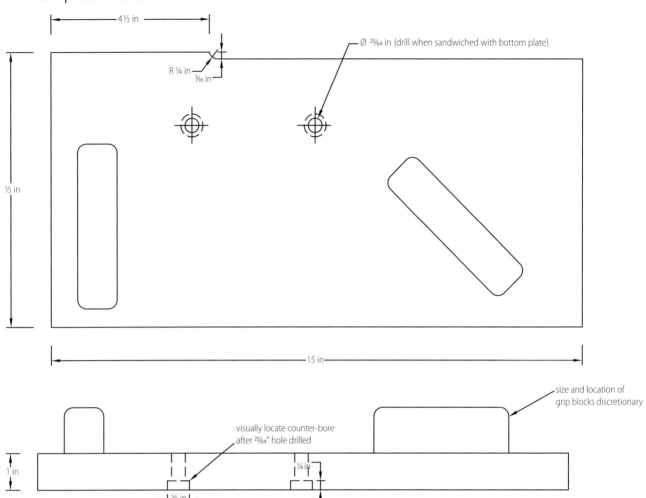

4 ½ in

R ¼ in
³⁄₁₆ in

Ø ²⁵⁄₆₄ in (drill when sandwiched with bottom plate)

½ in

15 in

size and location of grip blocks discretionary

visually locate counter-bore after ²⁵⁄₆₄" hole drilled

1 in

¼ in

⅝ in

B. Bottom Plate

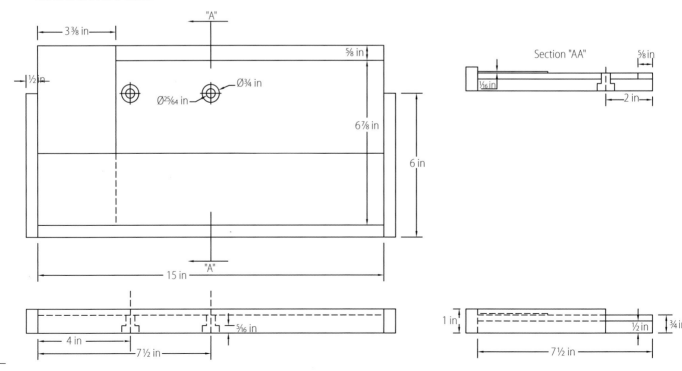

3 ⅜ in

"A"

⅝ in

½ in

Ø²⁵⁄₆₄ in   Ø¾ in

6 ⅞ in

6 in

15 in

"A"

4 in

7 ½ in

⁵⁄₁₆ in

Section "AA"

⅝ in

¹⁄₁₆ in

2 in

1 in   ½ in   ¾ in

7 ½ in

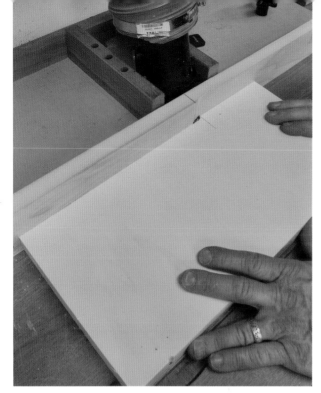

1. Place a pencil mark 4½" down from one end of the plate. Run the part past the set up until the cut reaches the pencil line.

2. Sand to shape with a small spindle sander set up.

The Template Plate

To get started, review the drawings for the ebony spline-shaping jig. As you can see there are basically two parts to the jig. The bottom plate positions the stock and registers the template plate. The template plate clamps down from the top to hold the blank immovable, while also serving as a contour template.

First, take two pieces of ½" plywood that are about 8" by 15½" and laminate them together to achieve the needed 1-inch thickness of the template plate. Next square up one corner of the glued up ply and cut it, as well as another piece of ½" ply (to be used later for the bottom plate) to 7½" x 15". Continue by setting up a router table with a ½" straight cutting bit and a fence that is offset by exactly ³⁄₁₆", the out-feed side being farthest out.

Adjust the out-feed side of the fence so it is flush with the top-dead-center of the router bit, the same as you would adjust the out-feed table of a jointer. If set up correctly, the stock should rest evenly and flat on both the in-feed and out-feed sides of the fence as it runs past the router bit. If this is not the case, re-adjust the top-dead-center alignment to the out-feed side of the fence. Place a pencil mark 4½" down from one end of the plate. Run the part past the set up until the cut reaches the pencil line. To finish off the template's shape, a ¼" radius is needed to smooth out the sharp corner left by the router bit cut. Use a Berol R-75 radius guide or other device to trace the radius, then sand to shape with a small spindle sander set up.

C. Template Plate Radiuses

A ¼" radius is needed to smooth out the sharp corner left by the router bit cut.

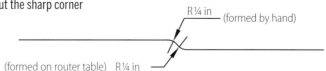

R ¼ in (formed by hand)

(formed on router table) R ¼ in

3. Attach MDF pieces to the bottom plate.

4. Laminate a ¹⁄₁₆" thick piece to the bottom plate.

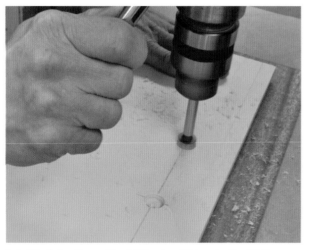

5. Drill both locations with a ¾" Forstner bit to a depth of ⁵⁄₁₆".

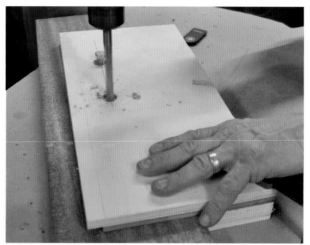

6. Clamp the plates together and drill two ²⁵⁄₆₄" holes.

7. With the plates still assembled, tack and glue the ½" x 1" material to the edge of the bottom plate.

8. Paint the surfaces that will come in contact with the stock with a non-skid coating.

D. Bottom Plate Pocket and Boring

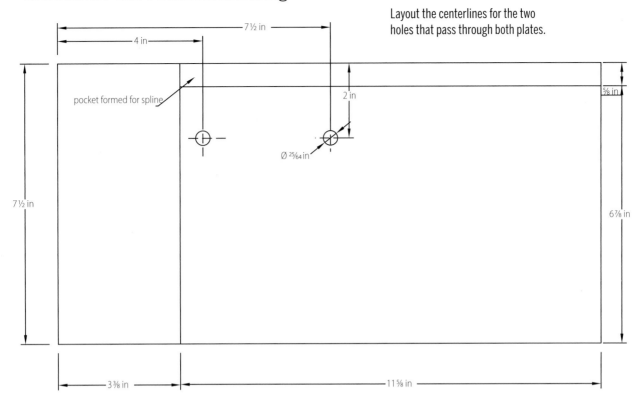

Layout the centerlines for the two holes that pass through both plates.

4 in

7½ in

pocket formed for spline

2 in

Ø ²⁵⁄₆₄ in

⁵⁄₈ in

7½ in

6⅞ in

3⅜ in

11⅝ in

The Bottom Plate

Set the template plate aside for now and go back to the ½" plywood (7½"x 15") that was cut out earlier for the bottom plate. Cut out two pieces of ¼" MDF, one at 3⅜" x 15½" and another at 6⅞" x 11⅝", and attach these to the bottom plate as seen in drawing D and photo 3. The blank space left will form a pocket to hold and register the spline stock.

Boring the Holes for the Bolts

Keep in mind that two ⅜" by 2" bolts will be used to hold the two plates together. It is important that their relative locations be precisely located. First, take a piece of material that is about ¹⁄₁₆" thick x 3" x 15" and laminate it to the bottom plate opposite the spline pocket. A good source for ¹⁄₁₆" material would be either plastic laminate or veneers of that thickness. Before going on, flush trim any material that might be overhanging the bottom plate. Now turn the bottom plate over so you are looking at the face opposite the laminations. Referring again to drawing D, layout the centerlines for the

two holes that pass through both plates. With a ¾" Forstner bit, drill both locations to a depth of ⁵⁄₁₆". Be sure to place some ¹⁄₁₆" material under the thinner portion of the plate for support.

Now, assemble the top and bottom plates together in their respective positions. Place a ¹⁄₁₆" spacer between the two plates where it is needed for support. Clamp the plates together and drill two ²⁵⁄₆₄" holes using the center drill point from the previous hole as registration points. A ⅜" bolt can be inserted into the first hole drilled to insure common registration.

With the plates assembled, clamp them together in a bench vice and tack and glue the ½" x 1" material to the edge of the bottom plate as shown in drawing B and photo 7. Next, using a non-skid coating material such as Skid-No-More by Evercoat, paint the surfaces that will come in contact with the stock, as shown in photo 8. Be sure to scrape away any material that may form in the corner of the bottom plate and prohibit correct registration of the stock.

9. Clean up the corners of the bottom plate.

10. Center and trace a ⅝" circle around the two holes.

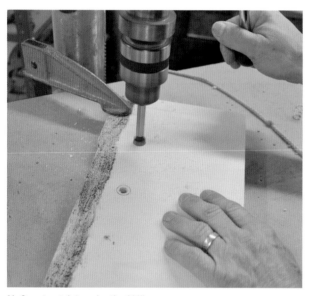

11. Countersink to a depth of ¼".

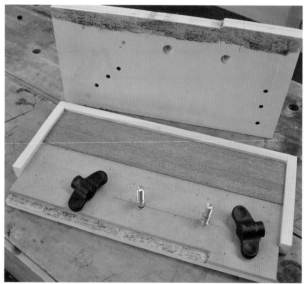

12. An inside view of the jig with compression springs in place.

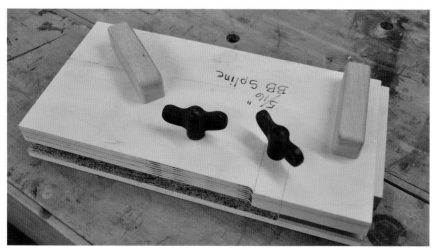

13. The finished jig.

E. The Slotting Jig

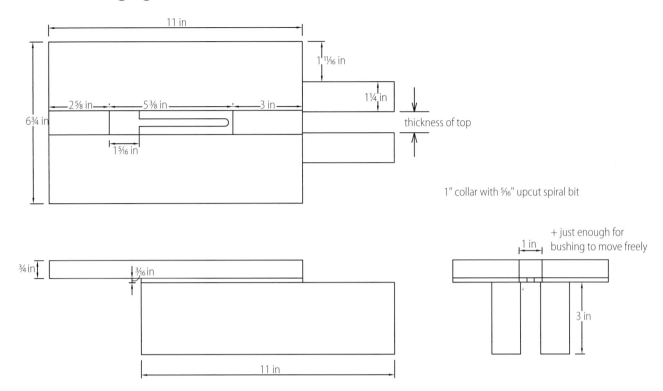

11 in

1 11/16 in

2 5/8 in · · 5 3/8 in · · 3 in

1 1/4 in

6 3/4 in

thickness of top

1 5/16 in

1" collar with 5/16" upcut spiral bit

3/4 in

3/16 in

+ just enough for
bushing to move freely

1 in

3 in

11 in

Going back to the inside face of the template plate, use a drafting guide to center and trace a 5/8" circle around the two holes. (This could have been done along with the other boring if I had not spaced out.) Visually registering the locations and using a 5/8" Forstner bit, countersink to a depth of 1/4".

Assembly

For the finishing touches, attach a couple of handles to the top of the template plate. Size and locate them in such a way that is comfortable to you. Next run two 3/8"x 2" hex head bolts from the bottom side of the bottom plate. The head of the bolt should recess and clear the bottom of the plate. Next place 3/4" x 1/2" compression springs over the bolts. The counter-bore on the inside face of the template plate will accept the compression springs when the jig is assembled. To finish the jig, place the template plate on the bolts and secure it to the bottom plate with two 3/8" wing nuts.

The Slotting Jig

This next jig is for routing the slot in the edge of the top for the ebony.

Cut out the following parts for the jig: two pieces of wood at 1" x 3" x 11", two pieces of 3/4" ply at 3" x 11", two pieces of 3/4" ply at just a hair over 1" wide and exactly 3" long, and one piece of 3/16" thick material 7" x 7 9/32". Sometimes 5mm ply can be found that is marketed as 1/4", but actually measures out at very close to 3/16". If stock material is not available then you will need to sand down some 1/4" MDF. (Tell your wife you need to buy a drum sander). Save small pieces of the 3/16" material for later use.

14. Dry-clamp the routing platform together and test a 1" bushing for ease of movement.

15. Assemble and glue the four pieces that make up the "routing platform."

16. Mark a line 1¹⁵⁄₃₂" down from the end of the opening.

17. Laminate the already cut out ³⁄₁₆" material to the face of the glued up parts, registering with the drawn line.

Clamp together the two pieces of ¾" x 3" x 11" ply with two small pieces of ¾" ply that are just a few thousands over 1" wide and exactly 3" long. Test fit a 1" router bushing for ease of movement in the opening formed between the larger pieces of ply. If necessary, re-size the small pieces of ply until the bushing moves easily with a minimum of slop.

Next, using biscuit or domino if available, glue the four pieces of ply together to form the "routing platform." The small 1" wide pieces should be flush with the ends of the larger pieces to form a 5½" open space in the middle.

Now, mark a line 1¹⁵⁄₃₂" down from the end of the opening, then register the already cut out ³⁄₁₆" material with the newly drawn line and attach it to the routing platform.

Theoretically the ³⁄₁₆" material should be flush with the two sides and the back end. If it overhangs at any point, flush trim it to the ¾" material.

Precise registration of the "clamping plates" to the "routing platform" is critical to the success of the jig. To accomplish this, take a ⅞" thick piece of wood (same thickness as the top) and sandwich and clamp it along with two pieces of printer

18. Use scrap material to fit flush along either side of the clamped assembly and flush with the outside edges of the platform.

19. Clamp the slotting jig to the stock and route a test groove.

paper between the two pieces of 1" x 3" x 11" wood (clamping plates) that were previously cut out. Now, place the clamped assembly on the backside of the routing platform and flush with the leading edge of the ³⁄₁₆" material. Measure for and cut two equal pieces of scrap material to fit flush along either side of the clamped assembly and flush with the outside edges of the platform, and then clamp the two pieces of scrap in position. Turn the clamped pieces over now and secure the routing platform to the clamping plates with about 3-4 wood screws each.

The clamping plates should now easily slip over the top and hold it securely in position with a single clamp. The resulting route should place a slot roughly in the center of the top's thickness.

Blanking out the Ebony Spline

With the jig making out of the way, we can now move on to making some progress on the detail itself. First, the exact width of the route produced by the slot jig needs to be determined so the ebony can be exactly sized. Set up a plunge router with a ⁵⁄₁₆" up-cut spiral bit and a 1" collar. Mill out some scrap stock to exactly ⅞" thick, which is the same thickness as the top. Clamp the slotting jig to the stock and route a test groove. Be sure to make two final passes; first with pressure on one side of the collar opening and another with pressure towards the other side. If you remove the router from the jig and then replace it and continue routing, make sure you note the router's orientation. If the router is turned side to side, any inaccuracy in the centering of the collar will cause the slot to enlarge.

Mill some scrap wood down in thickness until it produces a "light friction" fit in the test groove. With a satisfactory fit, and on the same thickness setting, mill out several more pieces of scrap, as well as the ebony, to a width of ⅝" and 5⅛" long. Mill one of the scrap pieces to about 1" wide. Leave the router set up with the ⁵⁄₁₆" bit and the 1" collar.

Using the Ebony Spline Shaping Jig

To start with, mark a line down the center of the thickness of the 1" wide scrap piece that was just cut out and register it in the corner pocket of the bottom plate. Secure the stock firmly with the wing nuts.

Next, in a router table, set up a full bullnose ½" radius bit with a ⅝" radius bearing (Amana # 51572). The center of the bit's radius must line up exactly with the center of the stock in the jig. Place a light source on the backside of the router table, then line up the jig so the line down the center of the stock centers itself on the crescent of light that defines the arc of the bit.

Be cautious when making the first router cut. If not done properly the jig can be grabbed and violently thrown. It is not necessary to route a path all the way to both ends of the jig. It is necessary only to clear, with a little margin, the normal pathway of the bit. If you have any apprehensions whatsoever ask for experienced help. Resting the jig firmly against the fence, pivot the jig into the cutter.

To make the initial cut, firmly rest the trailing end of the jig against the fence and then pivot into the cutter. The bearing should only make contact with the edge of the jig that faces the fence. If the bit grabs the leading edge that is not parallel with the fence it will most likely jerk and throw the jig.

The initial setting is unlikely to be perfectly centered. Examine the stock from the end to determine if the bit needs to be adjusted up or down to center the arc on the stock.

20. Center the stock and the bit.

21. To make the initial cut, firmly rest the trailing end of the jig against the fence and then pivot into the cutter.

22. Determine if the bit needs to be adjusted up or down.

23. Using one of the test pieces, trace the outline onto the ebony parts and band saw some of the extra material away.

With the bit height adjusted correctly, take one of the test pieces and trace the outline onto the ebony parts and band saw some of the extra material away. Be careful not to remove too much material from the ebony, just enough to reduce the chance of blowout. Now machine the ebony blanks and set them aside.

Making the Breadboard Top

The ebony spline detail is intended to visually enhance traditional breadboard construction. There are a number of suitable techniques used to construct the breadboards and you are free to use what works best for you. I will however, very briefly, cover the matter for those who would like some guidance.

The idea behind the breadboard is to control the warpage in solid wood construction. The technique takes advantage of the fact that wood is more likely to warp and move in the cross grain direction, and much less likely in the long grain direction. To put this in practice, a relatively narrow strip of solid wood (breadboard end) is attached with its long grain at a right angle to the solid wood panel (core) in its cross grain direction. The matter is complicated by the fact that the core will move across the joining point with changes in relative humidity, while the breadboard end will not.

To start, first route a ¼" x ½" deep slot (centered on the core thickness) in both the core and the breadboard end referencing from the bottom. In the core, glue in a ¼" x 1" wood spline with the grain following the direction of the core. The old rule of thumb allows for 4" of cross grain glue-up. With the center 4" of the breadboard end glued directly to the core, the core's movement is restricted from the center out. In other words, the core's movement will be controlled so it only moves half the total amount on either side. Further out from the center (every 4-6 inches— not evenly spaced per side but symmetrical from side to side), #10 x 2½" pan head wood screws are used to secure the end to the core. To allow the screws to move, leave about a ½" opening in the spline. Square and rectangular ebony plugs on the outside edge of the ends cover up the screw heads. Calculate the depth of the plug holes to allow the screw to penetrate the core (beyond the spline slot) to at least 1". To allow the screws to shift and flex as the core moves, pre-drill for the screws into the breadboard end, then counter bore with a ¼" bit leaving ¼–⅜" of meat. This method should be adequate for mahogany tops of less than 30" wide. For tops wider than 30" (more movement), make a lateral slot for the screw to move in.

The thickness and length of the breadboard end is dictated by the size of the core. The end is ⅛" thicker than the thickness of the core and ⅜" (³⁄₁₆" proud at either end) longer than the core is wide. The width of the end is normally between 2 ¼" and 2¾", but can be larger depending upon the scale of the design. When attaching the breadboard end to the core, use a piece of ³⁄₁₆" (the extra pieces set aside from building the routing platform) material to gauge the overhang.

All exposed corners of both the core and breadboard end are rounded over ⅛". When sanding, add a little extra softening to the

24. Pre-drill to allow the screw to flex.

radiused corners on the end-grain face of the breadboard end, giving it sort of a "worn" look.

When gluing the breadboard ends to the core, clamp the glued up center section, then one at a time, clamp near the screw locations and run the individual screws.

25. Glue the spline into the core leaving a ½" path for the screws, then glue the center 4" of the spline to the breadboard end.

Rounded "worn like" edges on the breadboard of the Thorsen server. William R. Thorsen House, 1909–10. Courtesy of the Gamble House.

26. When attaching the breadboard end to the core, use a ³⁄₁₆" spacer to gauge the amount of overhang.

27. Clamp and screw the end to the core.

28. Test the depth of cut.

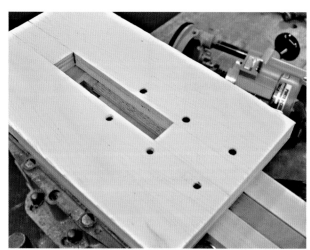

29. Register the ³⁄₁₆" material on the underside of the routing platform against the breadboard end.

30. Register the ³⁄₁₆" material against the breadboard end and clamp.

31. Register one face of a ⁵⁄₁₆" square hole punch (available at Lee Valley) square against the saddle with the opposite two points inside the slot.

Routing the Slot

First, the depth of cut must be determined. To do this, clamp the slotting jig to some ⅞" thick material and set the depth initially to roughly ⁵⁄₁₆" deep. Route a test slot, then test the depth with one of the ebony splines. Ideally about ¹⁄₁₆" of the shoulder should be showing.

With the depth set correctly, route the slots in the top. Be sure to register the ³⁄₁₆" material on the underside of the routing platform up against the

breadboard end. Next, the rounded ends of the routed slot need to be squared up.

Line up a Veritas Saddle Square, or a small square, precisely at the end point of the slot. Register one face of a ⁵⁄₁₆" square hole punch (available at Lee Valley) against the saddle with the opposite two points inside the slot. Push the two points of the punch nearest the saddle into the wood, remove the saddle, and drive the punch home with a steel hammer.

32. Using a steel hammer, drive the punch home.

33. Polish the face of the spline.

34. Mark the spline length.

35. Slightly back bevel the two ends.

Installing the Ebony Spline

Start by sanding the rounded face of the spline to 600-grit, while very slightly easing the corners. With white rouge polishing compound and a buffing wheel set up in the drill press, polish the face of the spline. Next line the spline up with the routed slot and mark the length of the slot on the narrow end of the spline. The wider end of the spline is already sized to suitably mimic the drop down from the breadboard end. Trim the spline to fit with a light ¹⁄₆₄" gap. Then ease and buff the just trimmed end. To avoid hanging up on the ends of the slot, slightly back bevel the two end faces. Next, in order to avoid bottoming out in the slot when the core contracts, relieve about ¹⁄₁₆" of material from the inside at the wide end.

Spread a little glue in the core side of the slot only. When the core expands and contracts the spline is designed to float in the breadboard end side of the slot; because of this, make sure no glue is applied there.

36. Tap the spline in place.

37. Position the ¹⁄₆₄" gap at the breadboard end side of the slot.

To finish off, tap the spline in place with a plastic headed mallet. Also, to aid in letting the spline float in the breadboard end side, position the ¹⁄₆₄" gap at that end.

Of the numerous Greene & Greene details emulated by today's woodworkers, the breadboard spline is among the most widely celebrated, and rightly so. It is a work of genius! It transforms the humble breadboard to the level of high art. It is something that begs to be touched and the silky smooth feel of polished ebony does not disappoint.

38. The ebony spline detail.

Chapter 6

The Strap Detail

The strap detail was used only one time by the Greenes for the Ford House letter case, which was a relatively small piece made to sit atop a writing table. The original detail was, in fact, an actual leather strap that ran under the cabinet from the front of the base to the back. I think it is safe to assume the original straps were meant to protect the tabletop from scratches.

The drawings for the letter case, dated February 25, 1908, did not include straps. This should not be considered unusual though. Greene & Greene furniture often differed from the design as originally drawn.

The Ford letter case in general, and the straps in particular, have held my interest for some time. A few years ago, I attempted to locate the piece for a firsthand look. In the process I tracked down several "leads" that included, among other things, a mysterious storage unit in the Southern California desert. Sometimes the story varied with the storage unit being located in Florida. Searching every storage unit in the

The Ford House letter case, c. 1908. Courtesy of the Gamble House.

Greene & Greene Style Blanket Chest by Darrell Peart showing strap detail.

southern California desert and the entire state of Florida were beyond my resources. I do hope that the piece does still exist somewhere though. Unfortunately, the two possible locations do not bode well, one being extremely dry and the other extremely humid.

Given that I could not find the actual piece of furniture, the next best thing would be the only known original archival photo of the piece, which appeared in Randell Makinson's book *Greene & Greene: Furniture and Related Designs*. Another dead end! The Greene & Greene archives had a record of the photo, but it was not in their possession and had been missing for some time. I had given up on even locating the photo until it was needed for a sidebar in a book that featured my blanket chest. After a renewed effort and numerous phone calls and emails, the original archival image was found mixed in with other papers. It is now back in the archives.

The primary reason I had exerted so much energy in locating the whereabouts of the original letter case was to acquire a better look at the straps, which had grabbed my imagination in a big way. Having only an archival black and white image to go on I could not see the detail as clearly as I would like. I could not even locate someone who had even as much as seen the original piece of furniture.

In an odd sort of way, it may have been good fortune that my search for the letter case did not pan out. Had I found it, I may not have relied so much upon my imagination when I decided to incorporate the detail into one of my designs.

So with my imagination employed I used visual analogies to help me design the strap, with my basic starting point being what I call "furniture DNA." It's not actual DNA, but rather "furniture building blocks" with which I play creator and lay down my own rules. Once the rules are laid down for a particular design those rules must permeate every detail as if it were nature's blueprint. In other words each detail has a purpose which relates back to and supports the overall design as a whole.

A. The Strap

The basic strap before sanding/shaping.

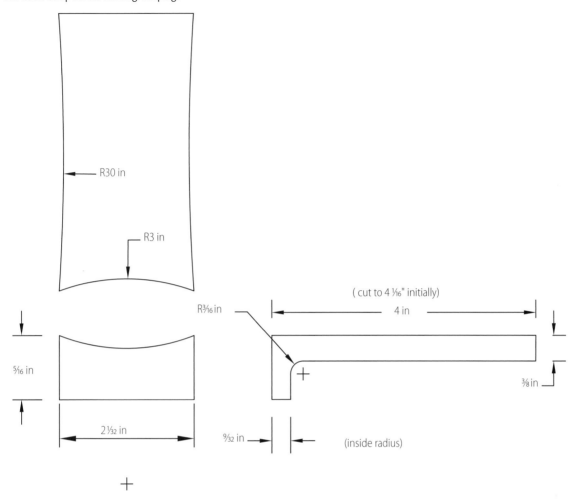

Visual weight plays a major role in my DNA scheme, with the strap detail serving to visually anchor the design to the ground (floor). To follow my train of thought you will need to rely upon your mind's eye. Imagine it's a couple of hundred years ago and you are at a dock where a cargo vessel is being loaded. The leather straps used to lift the heavy crates strain and stretch under their burden. To get to the next level in my scheme, your imagination has to do some serious heavy lifting as well. Think of the straps as agents in the employ of gravity. Instead of lifting upwards, they are pulling downward on the object that they have in their grasp. The straps are thus serving as anchors to secure the design to the floor. To determine placement of the straps, imagine the piece of furniture upside down and on the loading dock

again: where would the straps be placed in order to evenly balance the load for lifting?

The strap detail, as it plays out in my scenario, would only be used with designs that possess sufficient solid mass. A design with mostly negative space would not contain the mass needed for strapping. To understand this, transport yourself back to the loading dock again. The design is waiting to be loaded. Does its mass and weight require that it be up hoisted onboard with a pulley and straps or could you simply pick it up and walk up the plank with it?

Making the Straps

The strap detail is made from wood, but meant to give the impression of leather under stress. A natural material such as leather has at least small inconsistencies from one piece to the

B. Side Profile Jig

Jig for the strap's side profile.

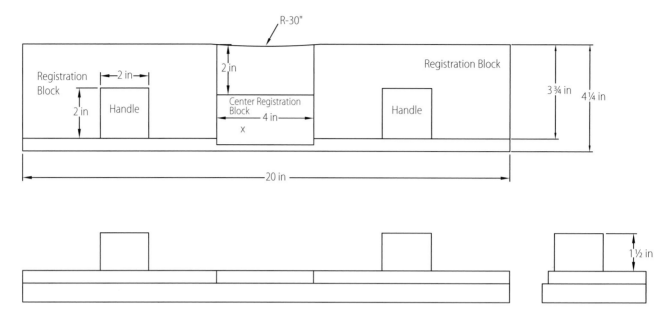

next. This is what gives it character. The goal then is for the wooden straps to exhibit some small inconsistencies. This is not an excuse for sloppy work though. There is plenty of room in the process that will produce minor irregularities without making an effort to do so. In other words, aim for consistency but be pleased that you don't quite reach it.

Blanking out the Material

The first order is to blank out the detail to a point that it can be further shaped by hand. Start by making the two jigs shown in drawings B and C. The registration blocks precisely capture the stock material for machining and care must be taken with their placement. Use screws without glue for the initial placement of the registration blocks; their position may need to be adjusted later. The precision of the radiused profile edges are not critical. Lay them out in pencil and simply sand to the line. With the jigs complete, set them aside for now.

For safety, as well as efficiency, mill out the stock in long lengths ¹⁵⁄₁₆" thick and 2¹⁄₃₂" wide. Two to four foot lengths are fine. The width must fit closely between the registration blocks of the top

profile jig. Make sure to cut out extra material to use for adjusting the setups.

Machining the Cove

Putting a cove down the center of the stock is the first step in shaping the strap. Start by raising the blade on the table saw to a height of ³⁄₁₆". Next take two pieces of the stock material and capture them (leaving an opening in between) with two pieces of straight scrap that are long enough to span the table saw top at a 45-degree angle. Also, between the scrap and stock material place single pieces of paper to hold the scrap a few thousands of an inch farther apart. Position the clamped assemblage at a 45-degree angle to the tabletop. Then moving the assemblage, find the spot where the teeth disappear into the throat plate evenly on either side of the opening. In other words, center the path of the blade from side to side while keeping the assemblage at 45-degrees.

With the saw set up, run a test piece through using push blocks. The resulting cut should be a cove that is exactly centered in the stock; if it is not, make the necessary adjustments. Once an acceptable cove is achieved, run all the stock and then cut them to 4¹⁄₁₆" lengths.

1. The blank stock must fit between the registration blocks of the top profile jig.

2. Take two pieces of the stock material and capture them (leaving an opening in between) with two pieces of straight scrap that are long enough to span the table saw top at a 45-degree angle.

3. Center the path of the blade, keeping the assemblage at 45-degrees.

4. Run a test piece through using pushes blocks.

5. The resulting cut should be a cove that is exactly centered in the stock.

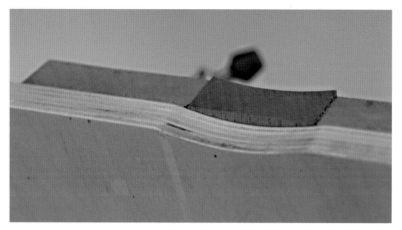

6. Place one of the blanks in the top profile jig.

7. Routing the strap stock.

The Top Profile

To emulate leather under stress, two arched profiles, top and side, will be routed into the blank. The next three steps (top profile route, inside radius, and side profile route) must be done in the order given.

To begin with, set up a top bearing flush trim bit in the router table. Going back to the top profile jig, mount two De-Sta-Co type toggle clamps for securing the stock. Next, place one of the blanks in the jig. The stock should over hang the front edge at the corners by 1⁄32"–1⁄16". If not, re-position the "registration handle" to correct it. With the jig set up correctly, route all the strap stock.

C. Strap Detail

Jig for shaping the top profile of the strap.

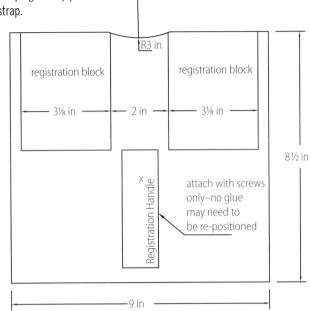

R3 in

registration block

registration block

3⅛ in | 2 in | 3⅛ in

8½ in

x

Registration Handle

attach with screws only–no glue may need to be re-positioned

9 in

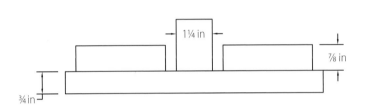

1¼ in

⅞ in

¾ in

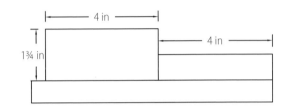

4 in

4 in

1¾ in

D. Push Blocks

Push block for routing the inside radius.

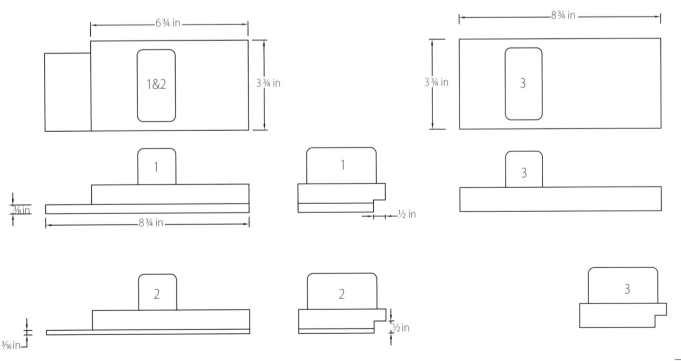

6¾ in

3¾ in

1&2

8¾ in

3¾ in

3

1

1

3

⅜ in

8¾ in

½ in

2

2

3

³⁄₁₆ in

½ in

3

8. Setting the core box.

9. Make three passes to minimize blow-out.

The Inside Radius

When finished, the strap will wrap around and attach to the base. I normally apply a ³⁄₁₆" radius to the top edge of my bases, which means the back inside corner of the strap must have a matching radius. If you choose to use a different radius for your base, change the following step accordingly.

First, set up a ³⁄₈" diameter (³⁄₁₆" radius) core box bit in a router table to a height of ⁹⁄₁₆" and ⁵⁄₁₆" back from the fence. I like to use a spiral bit because it is less likely to blow out the backside of the route, but a straight fluted bit will work as well. To further minimize the chance of blow-out, the ⁹⁄₁₆" depth should be taken in three incremental passes using push blocks similar to those shown in drawing D.

10. Routing for the backside radius.

11. Set the stock in the jig and check the overhang, which should be about ⅟₃₂.

Now, mount two De-Sta-Co style toggle clamps on the side profile jig and as before check that the stock slightly overhangs the routing profile. If necessary, reposition the "center registration block." To route, first clamp the stock in the jig and run one side, then flip the stock and run the opposite side.

12. Machine one side, then flip the stock and machine the opposite side.

13. Sand the top profile.

14. Sand the coved face.

15. Sand the top and bottom edges.

16. The top and bottom edges.

17. Trimming the blank.

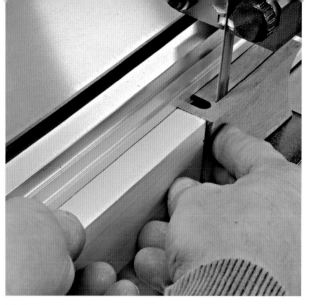
18. Use a push block.

19. Use a small stick or pencil to finish the cut.

20. The completed backside.

Preliminary Sanding and Shaping

Take the opportunity now, before the stock is cut, to sand and lightly shape the piece. Set up a spindle sander with a four-inch (or the largest spindle available) spindle. Sand both the top profile and the coved face to take out the machine marks. With a pivoting motion lightly roll over the top edge as well as the bottom edge.

Band Saw to the Inside Radius

For the next step, place one of the blanks on the band saw with the backside (flat side) against the fence and visually line up the tangent point of the inside radius with the blade. Using a push block, run the stock with the flat side against the fence and the straight end first into the blade. Stop when the cut reaches the tangent point. Use a small stick or pencil to push the wasted material on through the saw. If the cut is not within about 1/64" of the tangent point, adjust the fence and try again with another piece of stock. Repeat this until the cut is satisfactory, and then run all the parts.

21. Sand the strap until the backside is smooth and even.

22. Smooth out all the sharp edges.

Sand the Backside to Perfect Shape

The backside of the strap can now be fine-tuned so it wraps around the base flawlessly. First find a piece of scrap that is about 6" wide and 8" long, or larger. Along one corner of the edge route a ⅛" radius. Starting with the radiused edge, wrap a lengthwise section, 6 inches or so, of the scrap piece with adhesive backed (PSA) 80-grit sandpaper. With the added thickness of the sandpaper, the ⅛" radius will now mimic closely the ³⁄₁₆" radius on the actual base. Clamp the sandpapered scrap piece in a bench vise, then using a back and forth motion, sand the strap until the backside is smooth and even. When sanding the strap, be sure to position it so it rests consistently in the same plane as it is moved back and forth. In other words do not let it rock on its axis.

Blending to Shape

The basic shape of the strap now needs to be smoothed and blended to its final shape. Again, the end purpose here is to produce something that loosely mimics leather, a natural substance. Exact copies are neither the goal nor even desirable.

23. Soften the four corners.

The general idea is to heavily soften all the sharp edges and corners. To start, cut a piece of scrap material into approximately a three-inch cube. Radius all the corners on one face and then attach it to another piece of scrap about three inches wide and nine inches long. Clamp the assembled fixture to the bench then stretch a piece of 80-grit PSA paper over the face of the cube. The fixture will be used to hold and steady the strap while it is being shaped. With 80-grit sandpaper held in your palm, and backed by your

24. If it is more than ¹⁄₁₆", roughly trim the excess overhang on the band saw.

25. Sanding for a perfect fit.

thumb, use a sort of flapping motion to smooth out all the sharp edges. Put a little extra emphasis on the softening at the four corners, but not so much as to lose the appearance of stretched leather. Once the shape is basically established, finish the sanding by touching up and blending where necessary. Continue sanding through the grits up to 220, and 320 on the end grain at the top corner.

Fitting the Strap to the Base

When I first made the strap detail, there were no instructions to help me. I had to make it up as I went along. This went fairly well until I needed to trim the overhang to precisely match the corresponding distance at the top of the base. Although near the floor, the detail is unusual and at some point it will, hopefully, capture the viewer's attention, which in turn will likely lead to a closer inspection. The view will be from overhead, looking directly down on the point where the trimmed overhang meets with the case or pedestal. Even the slightest gap will be painfully conspicuous. A perfect fit is essential and at first this eluded me. The problem is, no

matter how diligent and precise you are, you will never be able to consistently align the base with the case or pedestal so that it is the same, within a few thousands of an inch all around the entire perimeter. In other words, there is no uniformity to rely upon. Each individual strap placement must be custom fitted.

Like most woodworking problems, the seemingly difficult solution was surprisingly simple once it was solved. To precisely fit the strap, first estimate how much material needs to be trimmed. If it is more than ¹⁄₁₆ of an inch, back up the strap overhang with a push block to trim the excess off on the band saw. Next, apply a narrow strip of 80-grit PSA sandpaper to the strap location at the point on the case or pedestal where it meets with the overhang. Measure the thickness of the PSA sandpaper with Vernier calipers. Now find an equivalent thickness of paper, which usually equals about two thicknesses of card stock. Tape the measured paper to the base just below the PSA sandpaper. Next, with the strap in position, slide it back and forth letting the 80-grit sandpaper remove material from the overhang until it ceases to

26. Position and glue the strap in place.

27. The finished strap detail.

remove anything. The measured paper should have allowed the sandpaper to remove precisely the amount of material to form a perfect fit. If a small gap appears (too much material removed) you may have placed too much pressure on the topside of the strap. Even sanding pressure should be given on the overhang of the strap where it rests on the face of the base.

Attaching the Strap to the Base

First, make a clamping caul by tracing the coved shape of the strap on a block of wood roughly the same width and length as the strap itself.

Cut the shape out on the band saw and smooth out any inconsistencies on an edge sander, and then attach a soft material, such as leather, to the face. Before clamping, the piece of furniture being worked on must be elevated with blocks so a clamp can reach in behind the base. Next using a small amount of glue, position the strap in place, and clamp it using the newly made caul.

The strap detail was an inspired feature. Although the Greenes never used it in same manner as I have, I believe it lends itself well to the style. As always, use it in context, but do not be afraid to experiment and have fun with it.

Chapter 7

The Waterfall Leg

The Greenes (most likely Charles) maintained complete control over even the smallest of details in a design. Even a minor component such as the waterfall leg had a purpose beyond its first impression. Nothing was superfluous. Everything had a reason and was fine-tuned to its specific situation. Their artistic vision for a design was complete, with virtually no loose ends. In other words, every detail in a piece of furniture worked in complete harmony to support the design as a whole. Every element had its own measured contribution to the common good. There were no freeloaders! This did not happen with a few select designs; it permeated almost everything they did.

The Greenes employed an infinite number of design elements, such as the waterfall detail, in their work. Sometimes the ideas were original and other times they were borrowed. But they did not simply copy and paste a borrowed idea. They not only infused it with G&G DNA, but each specific use was given careful consideration. Context was central to even the smallest of details.

From my viewpoint, there are many classic end-of-leg design features that either amplify or diminish the overall weight of a piece. Tapering the two inside faces at the bottom of a leg, as is seen in the waterfall detail, is a classic trick used to contain and transfer the visual weight of a design to the point of contact with the floor

The Gamble master bedroom game table with more visual weight. David B. Gamble House, 1908-09. Courtesy of the Gamble House.

The game table's waterfall detail with the longer first step. David B. Gamble House, 1908-09. Courtesy of the Gamble House.

The side chair from the Gamble House (1908) master bedroom had less visual weight than the game table. David B. Gamble House, 1908-09. Courtesy of the Gamble House.

(point of gravity). The Greenes used this device in at least a couple of incarnations, but with the Gamble house master bedroom it reached its full assimilation into the family of Greene & Greene. Here the detail was genetically re-engineered and given a new life. Instead of a simple straight taper line, the Greenes added a couple of gentle uneven soft steps. It was not just simply re-engineered and then replicated—it was adapted for each specific situation.

I love to work out analogies in my head to explain designs. These ideas are entirely my own musings and I do not want to suggest that I have by some means "channeled" the mind of Charles Greene. I wish I could!

One of my favorite analogies involves the treatment of visual weight and strength. These two facets of design—weight and strength—are symbiotic and play parallel functions within my analogy. When weight is increased, additional strength is needed for support. When strength is amplified, the apparent weight of the design increases. Strength and weight can also be seen as, masculine equals heavy and strong while feminine is analogous to lighter and more delicate. For the purpose of simplification, though, I generally only use the term "visual weight."

In my last book, I described another bottom of the leg treatment, the "Blacker leg indent." In that case, I asked my readers to imagine the visual weight of the piece pushing down on

The side chair had a shorter first step than the game table. David B. Gamble House, 1908-09. Courtesy of the Gamble House.

and residing in the very bottom portion of the leg, past the indent. In the case of the waterfall detail, although it's still visual weight at play, the scenario works out a bit differently. Instead of containing the weight of the piece, the waterfall serves to transfer and dissipate the visual weight to the floor.

Charles nuanced the detail to suit each particular use. It is not known what determining factors guided Charles Greene. It may or may not have been something parallel to my analogy. It may have been simply based on the overall length of the leg. We will never know. Nonetheless, I believe my visual weight theory serves to illustrate, at least in my mind, how the detail relates back to the overall design. I would

encourage my readers to take the time to follow my analogy though. It may not work for you, but in going through the exercise you may gain an understanding that will aid in developing your own analogies.

There are two constants in the waterfall's equation: the overall length and the lengths of each individual step. No matter what else is going on with the design, these things remain the same. The two individual steps were not equal in length though. One was unquestionably longer than the other. In the designs with more visual weight, such as the game table, the first step was the longest, and in those with less visual weight, such as the side chair, the steps were reversed. Please follow along as the analogy plays out.

Picture for a moment if you will, the visual weight of the piece pushing down upon the lower legs. There is a given space in which to make all the weight transfer happen. But secondary to that, imagine that initially this weight transfer must be reduced to a manageable load before it engages the second and final step. The designs with more weight in play will require more space (length) initially to reduce the weight to that point of manageability. With this set of rules in place the more "weighty" designs will have the longer step first. And for the "less weighty" pieces the reverse is true.

Another piece in the room, the night table, features a reverse tapered leg with a "pointy" end at the bottom of the waterfall detail. I have no doubt there was a reason for the variations on this piece. Again, the real reason can only be answered by the Greenes (Charles). For this we would need a time machine, and for the present I find myself without one. So until then, we can only continue to speculate and form analogies and theories.

Laying Out the Templates

The waterfall detail is fairly simple to make. We will go through the process of making both versions: one with the short step on the bottom, labeled "(A)", and one with the long step on the bottom, labeled "(B)".

To start with, cut two pieces of ¾" good quality plywood to exactly 4½" wide by about 20" long. The 20" length will accommodate a 17" long leg and allows for a two-inch lead-in at the beginning of the template and a one-inch run-out at the end. If your leg is longer than 17", adjust the overall length accordingly. If you only plan on making one of the waterfall configurations, you will only need to cut out one piece of template stock.

A. Waterfall Leg Detail

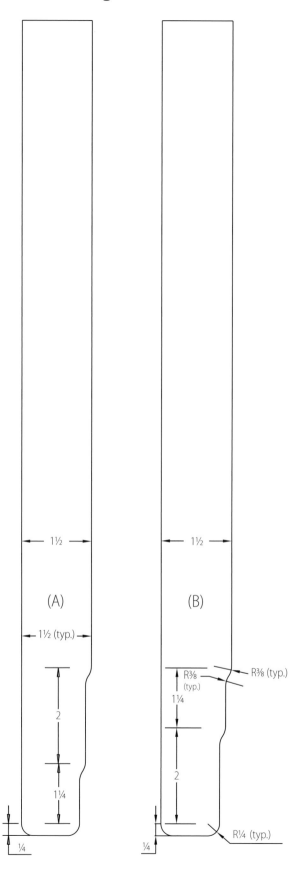

1. Lead-in and starting points for each step.

2. First offset the fence by ⅛".

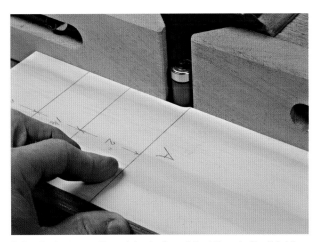

3. Run both pieces of template stock past the bit, up to the third line.

4. Re-adjust the infeed side to ¼" back from the outfeed side.

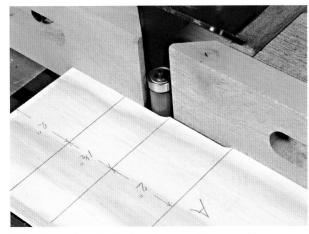

5. Run the stock again, this time stopping at the second line.

Referring to drawing B (page 79), draw the three lines that represent the lead-in and starting points for each step.

Note that the dimension for the first, lower, step also includes the ¼" round-over portion at the bottom of the leg.

Next, set the router table up with a ¾" (⅜"radius) straight bit. Offset the fence so the out-feed side is tangent with the bit and the in-feed side is set back from the out-feed side by exactly ⅛", then run both pieces of template stock past the bit, up to the third line. Now re-adjust

6. Draw the mating outside radius.

7. Sand up to the pencil line.

8. Flush the block to the back of the template.

9. The finished routing templates.

the in-feed side so it is ¼" back from the out-feed side. Run the stock again, this time stopping at the second line. The stopping points of the two cuts have formed the needed ⅜" inside radius of both steps.

Next, draw the mating outside radius. Using any object with a ⅜" radius (Berol RapidDesign R-75 shown), connect tangentially the inside radius with the intersecting straight line. With a spindle sander, carefully eat away the material up to the pencil line. The lines are small and just for general reference. Be careful not to remove too much material—usually just a light touch is sufficient.

Attaching the Registration Blocks to the Template

Before attaching the registration blocks, orient the template so that when facing up, the "steps" are on your right. This positions the jig to cut "downhill" rather than into the grain and reduces considerably the chances of blowout. Next, fasten a block to the "lead in" side of the first line (refer to drawing B). This block registers the bottom of the leg.

Now fasten a block that is about 1 ½" thick x exactly 3" wide x about 16" long to the template. Flushing the block to the back of the template should situate the block exactly 1½" back from the face edge of the template. The set back is critical,

B. Waterfall Routing Templates

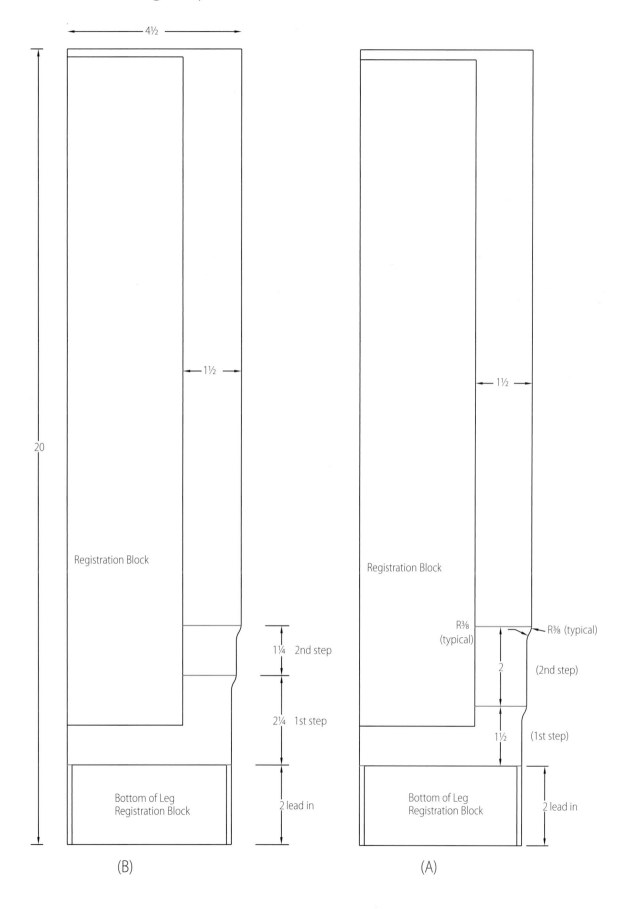

10. Register the leg stock in the template and trace the waterfall steps.

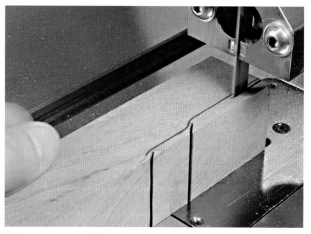

11. Band saw some of the excess material away.

so adjust the block's placement if necessary. Finish off by mounting two toggle clamps to the templates.

Machining the Leg

Machine the leg stock to 1⁹⁄₁₆" x 1⁹⁄₁₆" x (your needed length). The finished legs will be 1½" x 1 ½", but they are blanked out oversize to allow for a full profile cut, which ensures a smooth transition from the straight line to the routed steps. Now, set up the router table with a top bearing ¾" (⅜ radius) flush trim bit. Register the leg stock in the template and trace the waterfall steps, then, staying away from the line, bandsaw some of the excess material away. Clamp the stock back in the template and route the profile starting from the left (top of the leg) and ending the cut on the right (bottom of the leg). Rotate the stock 90 degrees counterclockwise and repeat the process to complete the routing.

Sanding and Shaping

A few key points to keep in mind before we start on the final round-over shaping and sanding. These concepts can be applied, with very few exceptions, to most any Greene & Greene shaping and softening applications. A round-over should present a seamless transition from the flat

12. Place the stock in the template and route the profile.

14. Clean up the chatter left over from routing the steps.

13. Shape the perimeter of the bottom end of the leg.

15. Soften the round-over between the individual steps.

surface to the radiused edge. Viewing the round over from different light angles will highlight any discrepancies in the smooth transition. Progressing through the grits on the flat surfaces will slightly diminish the round-overs, making minor sanding/shaping corrections necessary. Be cautious however, to not sand/shape too aggressively. The final touches are best done with a very light touch, while paying close attention to how the sanding is affecting the shape.

To begin the round-over process, set up a router table with a zero-clearance ¼" radius round over bit. Use this setup to shape the perimeter

of the bottom end of the leg. Next, round-over all four edges down the length of the leg with a ⅛" radius bit. The back corner where the waterfall steps meet cannot be done with the router and will be sanded to shape later.

Starting with 120-grit sandpaper wrapped around a flexible sanding pad, clean up the chatter left over from routing the profile. Make sure to sand right up to and including the inside radius of the step. Continue on with the sanding pad, using a backward drawing motion to evenly sand and soften the outside radius of the step-down. Progress though the grits up to 220.

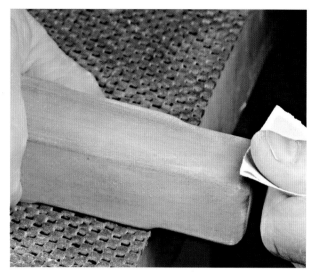

16. Sand and shape the ¼" round over at the bottom of the leg.

17. Draw down the corners of the round-over.

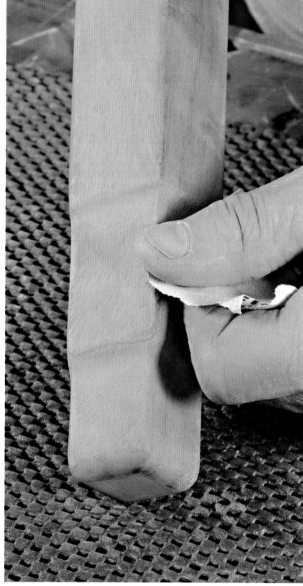

18. Shape an ⅛" radius on the sharp edge where the steps meet on the backside.

Sand the four long faces of the leg and their adjoining ⅛" radiuses. Error on the side of slightly enlarging the round-over rather than leaving it diminished. Now, starting with 120-grit sandpaper backed up by your thumb, use a flapping motion to sand and shape the ¼" round over at the bottom of the leg. Use the same flapping motion to draw down the corners of the round-over.

Again, starting with 120-grit, finish off the waterfall detail by shaping about a ⅛" radius on the sharp edge where the steps meet on the backside.

19. The waterfall leg detail in the "B" configuration.

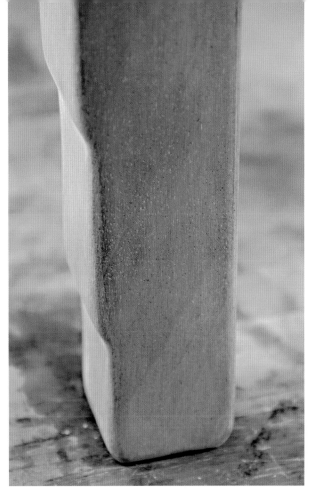

20. The waterfall leg detail in the "A" configuration.

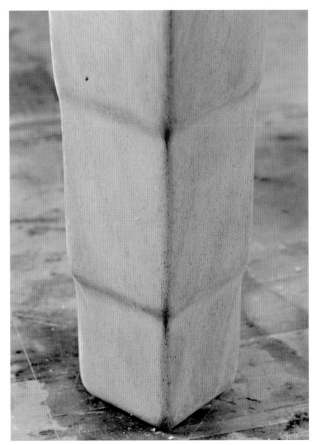

21. The detail changes character when seen from the backside.

The waterfall detail is deceptively simple. With just a bit of "tweaking," the Greene's adapted it to complement changes from one design to the next. Use it and adapt it, but give careful consideration to its specific use. As with any design element, context is all-important.

Chapter 8

Speaker Stands

I have been combining my interest in audio gear and woodworking for many years. Back in the early 70s, I was employed making large laminated beams. The end cuts and trimmed pieces could be quite large, measuring several feet long and as much as five feet wide and a foot or more thick. With a little stain and some cinder blocks, these would become a stand to proudly display my stereo gear.

Over the years my efforts at audio related furniture has become a bit more sophisticated. The Greene & Greene style speaker stands are my latest effort in that regard and the first time in many years that I have designed and made something for personal use.

A new design element introduced with this piece is what I am calling "rafter tails." Their relationship to Greene & Greene architecture is evident, but in this case my rafter tails are not supporting a roof structure, but instead a set of vintage speakers.

As you can see, the upturn in the rafter tails is sized to jut out uniformly from the speaker, and also extend out from each leg an equal distance. I have sized my stands specifically for a pair of AR-10pi's, my favorite vintage speakers. You will need to do a little math to size the stands to your speakers.

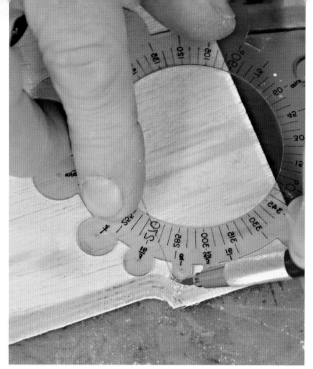

1. Along one long edge mark a line 1³⁵⁄₆₄" down from the end.

2. Use a ⅛" radius guide to draw in the upturn transition.

Getting Started

To start with, let's finish off the cut-list and get the math out of the way. First, measure the footprint of your speakers. For the length of the rafter tails (both side and front/back dimensions), add four inches. For the rails, subtract 4½" front and side.

The above formula is based on using floating tenons throughout the project. If you choose to use a traditional mortise and tenon instead, be sure to add the length of the tenons back into the calculations.

With the cut-list complete, proceed to blank out all of the parts for both stands. Be sure to run a few extra pieces of scrap at the same time to use later for setups.

Making the Shaping Templates

To construct the rafter tail template, first cut a piece of ¾" MDF or plywood to about 11" x 18". Referring to drawing A, mark a line 1³⁵⁄₆₄", using an Incra rule or similar accurate marking tool, down from one end. Next, set up a router table with a ½" (¼"radius) straight bit and offset the out-feed side of the fence by ¼". Set the out-feed side of the fence flush with the cut of the bit. If set up correctly, the material should rest flat on both the in-feed and out-feed sides as it passes by the bit. Along one long edge, mark a line 1³⁵⁄₆₄" down from the end, and then run the template stock to the line. This establishes a ¼" radius at the start of the upturn on the topside of the rafter tails. Use a ⅛" radius guide to draw in the upturn transition.

Cut List—2 each Rafter Tail Speaker Stands					
Qty.	Description	Material	Thick	Wide	Long
8	Legs	Khaya	1¾	1¾	13¹¹⁄₁₆
4	Front/Back Top Rails	Khaya	¾	1¾	Speaker Front/Back Minus 4½"
4	Front /Back Lower Rails	Khaya	¾	1	Speaker Front/Back Minus 4½"
4	Side Top Rails	Khaya	¾	1¾	Speaker Sides Minus 4½"
4	Side Lower Rails	Khaya	¾	1	Speaker Sides Minus 4½"
4	Front Facing Rafter Tails	Khaya	¾	1⁹⁄₁₆	Speaker Front/Back Plus 4"
4	Side Facing Frater Tails	Khaya	¾	1⁹⁄₁₆	Speaker Sides Plus 4"
16	Floating Tenons Top Rails	Any	⅜	1¼	1⁹⁄₁₆
16	Floating Tenons Lower Rails	Any	⅜	⅝	1¹⁵⁄₁₆

A. Greene & Greene Style Speaker Stands

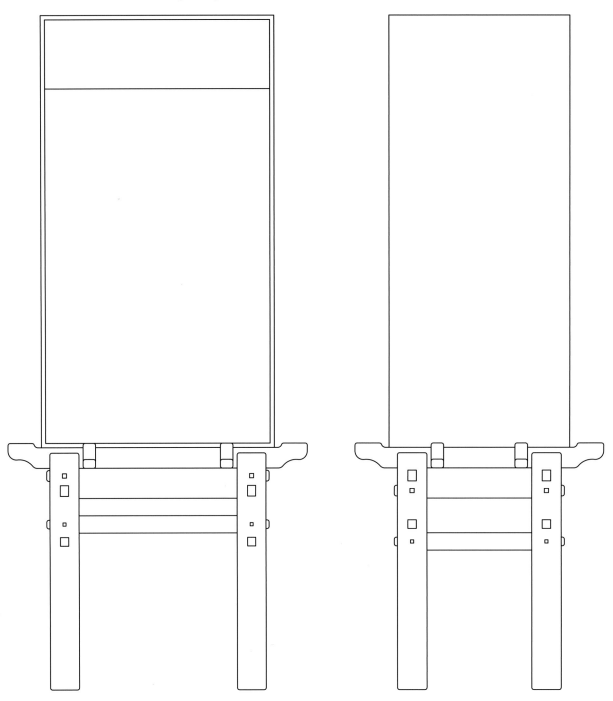

B. Top Side Template Route

Along one long edge mark a line 1³⁵⁄₆₄" down from the end.

R¼ in

1³⁵⁄₆₄ in

3. Then sand the corner to the penciled shape.

4. Pencil both arcs in.

5. Draw in the radius that tangentially connects the two smaller arcs.

6. Band saw close to the line, and then use a spindle sander to finish up.

Then sand the corner to the penciled shape with a spindle sander.

Next, at the same end but on the opposite corner (reference drawing D), layout the center marks for the radiuses for the bottom side of the rafter tail ends. Using a radius guide again, pencil in both the ⅜" and ½" radiuses. To mark in the connecting 1³⁄₆₄" radius, use the inside circle of the radius guide. To put shape to the line, band saw close to the line, then use a 2" spindle sander to sand to the final shape.

Now, attach two registration/clamping blocks (approximately ¾" x 4" x 18") to the template. Refer to the drawing for block placement and orientation. The setback is very important as it

relates to the final sizing of the parts. The given orientation allows the stock to be flush trimmed with a minimum chance of blowout. Next, fasten a stop block flush to both the end of the top profile and the template's routing edge. To finish off the routing template, mount two De-Sta-Co type clamps on each side for securing the stock.

Machining the Rafter Tails
The rafter tails are held together in a grid configuration with an interlocking half-lap joint. To start with, set up a dado head in the table saw set to cut just a few thousands over the width of the stock (¾"+). Using a sled to make the first cut on scrap material, set the height to ²⁵⁄₃₂" and the

7. The finished routing template.

8. Using a sled with a dado head to make the cut for the interlocking half-lap joint.

cut to start 4 ½" in from the end. When two pieces of scrap have been dadoed, assemble the joint. They should push together without much force and when bottomed-out the two pieces should be dead level. Once a good cut is achieved, proceed to run all the rafter tail parts.

To flush trim the parts using the shaping template, first set up a ½" top bearing flush trim bit in a table router. Keep in mind that in order for the half-lap interlocking joint to work, one set of rafter tails must orient with the dadoed cut up while the other orients with the dado cut down. It does not matter which group is oriented up or which group is oriented down, just as long as both sides are the same and both front/back pieces are the same.

To shape the rafter tails, start with the bottom side of the profile. Band saw to within ⅟₁₆" or so and then clamp the stock in the jig with one end of the stock flush with the end of the template. With the end of the template resting on a safety guide pin or suitable stable object (such as a fence, as shown in the photo), start the cut by pivoting into the router bit somewhere close to the center of

9. With the end of the template resting on a stable object, start the cut by pivoting into the router bit somewhere close to the center of the piece.

C. Top Side with Transition Radius

The ⅛" radius upturn transition.

R¼ in

R⅛ in

D. Bottom Side Radius Layout

The center marks for the radiuses for the bottom side
of the rafter tail ends.

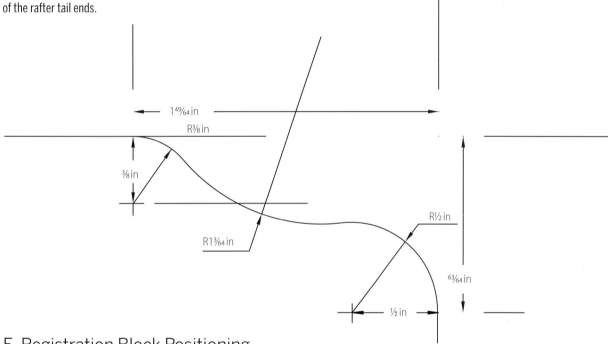

1⁴⁹⁄₆₄ in

R⅜ in

⅜ in

R1³⁄₆₄ in

R½ in

⁶³⁄₆₄ in

½ in

E. Registration Block Positioning

The rafter tail routing template with registration
block placement.

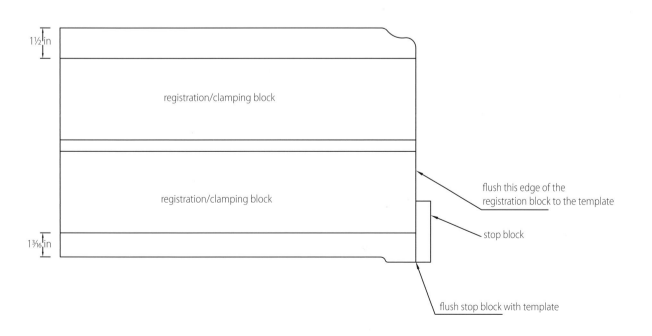

1½ in

registration/clamping block

registration/clamping block

flush this edge of the
registration block to the template

stop block

1³⁄₁₆ in

flush stop block with template

10. To start the top profile cut, rest the router bearing first against the end of the stop block.

11. Put a ⅛" round-over on all edges, stopping short of the half lap joint.

the piece. Take the piece out and reverse it to route the other end. If you start the secondary route in an area where the cut has already been made there is no need to go through the pivot procedure.

To route the top profile, first band saw to within about 1/16" of the actual cut, then clamp the stock in the template with the end referenced against the stop block. To start the cut, rest the router bearing first against the end of the stop block, then proceed to route about half of the distance of the profile. Flip the part end for end and route the other half.

Next, put a ⅛" round-over on all edges stopping short of the half-lap joint. With a sanding block and 150-grit sandpaper, lightly knock down the outermost top side corner of the rafter tail profile, and then blend it in by hand also with 150-grit. Sand all the parts to 220-grit, making a special effort to lightly soften and blend all corners.

Assembling the Rafter Tails

Before gluing up, dry-fit all the parts. If everything went as planned, the pieces should fit together and still level out when the joint is bottomed-out. If this is not so, you will have to either shim the joint or clean it out with a chisel to compensate.

To glue up, lightly spread glue in the dadoed joints and simply clamp the parts together. With a hand held router, go back and route the remaining ⅛" round-overs leading up to the crisscrossed joints.

Machining the Legs and Rails

With two sets of legs, it is very easy to become confused and place a mortise in the wrong location. To avoid this, mark the top of the legs with arrows pointing in towards the center and label each leg as to its relative orientation: LF (left front), RF (right front), RR (right rear), LR (left rear).

F. Rafter Tail Dado Layout
The location of the inter-locking tail lap joints.

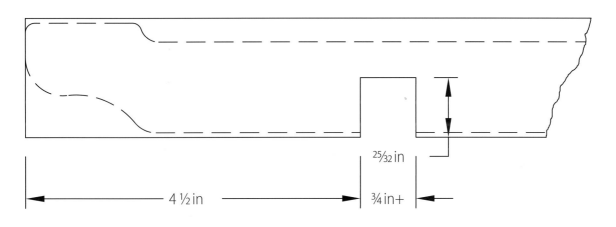

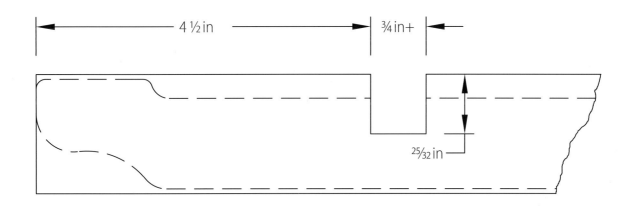

G. Leg Orientation
Each leg labeled with its orientation.

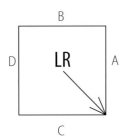

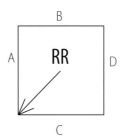

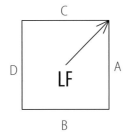

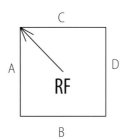

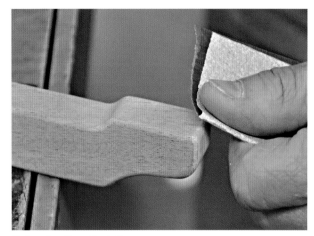
12. Sanding the rafter tail.

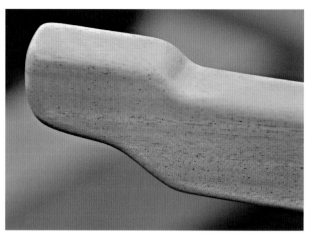
13. Lightly soften and blend all corners.

14. Lightly spread glue in the dadoed joints and simply clamp the parts together.

15. Label each leg as to its relative orientation: LF (left front), RF (right front), RR (right rear), LR (left rear).

Referring to drawing H, layout the locations for the mortises and square plug holes. Machine the mortises in both the legs and the rails using whatever method you are comfortable with. To make the ebony plug holes, refer to Chapter 4. The mortises on faces "A" and "C" are for the actual working joinery. Machine all the 1 ¼" long mortises to a depth of ⅝" and all the ⅝" long mortises to a depth of 1". Machine all the mortises in the rails to a depth of 1" (drawing I). These mortises can be left with round ends if your method produces them that way. The mortises on faces "B" and "D" are for the faux exposed tenons; machine these to a depth of about ½". For the square holes ½", ¼" and ³⁄₁₆", simply use a Lee Valley square punch (see Chapter 4). For the rectangular holes, you can start with a square hole (as above) that is centered along the length of the hole, and then use the punch to gain the needed length (again, see Chapter 4). Or, if you are using a multi-router, or similar machine as I am, you will need to square up the round corners for the rectangular, exposed holes. To do this, use a ½" square punch and register it with a small square or "saddle." Referring to the cut list, you can now mill the floating tenon stock (unless you are employing traditional tenons). If your mortises have rounded ends, use a router table with a fence to put a ³⁄₁₆" radiused profile on the edge of the tenon stock.

H. Leg Mortises and Holes

Layout the locations for the mortises and square plug holes.
All mortises/holes centered on width.

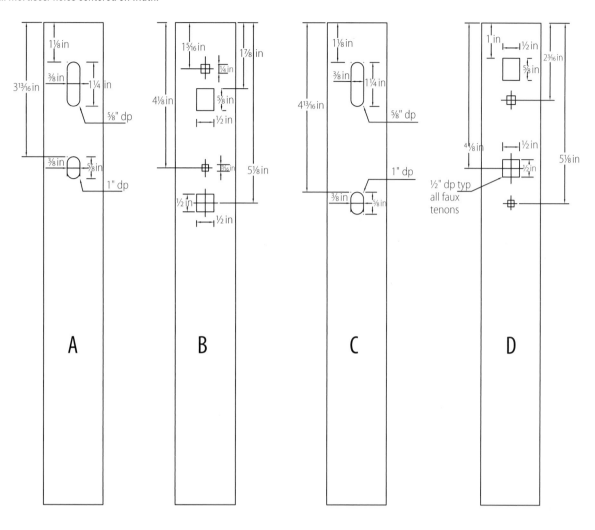

I. Rail Mortises

All mortises/tenons centered on end of rails.

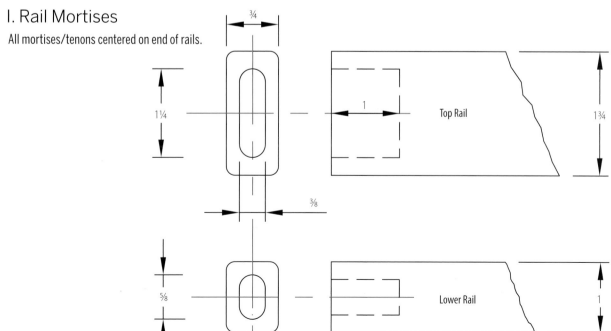

16. Using the square punch to square up the faux tenon hole.

17. The "worn" look.

18. Joining two legs with the top rail spaced ⅞" down.

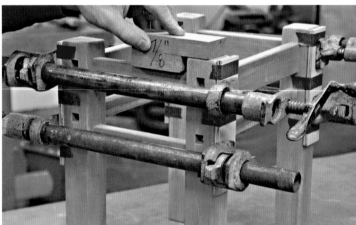
19. Join the two halves together.

With the machining out of the way, all exposed edges can be rounded over with a ⅛" radius. Next, sand all parts to 220-grit and pay special attention to smoothing out any defining lines left at the corner round-overs. When sanding the top of the legs, slightly draw down the four corners where three lines converge, giving it sort of a "worn" look.

Assembly

Before assembling, make a spacer block that is exactly ⅞" thick and attach a piece of scrap to its top so it forms an inside corner that can be used to verify the ⅞" set-down of the top rail from the top of the leg. Dry fit all the parts, first using the spacer block. The glue up is much easier if done in smaller manageable steps. Start by joining the front two legs to their respective rails, followed by the rear two legs and their rails, both as separate

operations. To finish off the glue-up, simply join the two halves together.

Faux Tenons

To make and insert the ³⁄₁₆" and ¼" ebony plugs, refer to Chapter 4. Next, machine the faux tenon stock out in long rods that are about 15-thousands (roughly ¹⁄₆₄") over the size of the opening. Measure each rectangular hole for consistency and adjust the sizes of the faux tenon stock if needed.

To put shape to the exposed ends of the faux tenons, first put a ⅛" round-over around the perimeter of the end. Then, with the stock clamped in a vice, mark a pencil line down the center of the end. Starting with 150-grit and, using a seesaw motion, sand until the pencil mark is gone. Keep the motion somewhat shallow in order to leave some of the ⅛" round-over. Next, use the

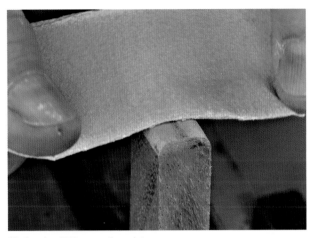

20. Sand until the pencil mark is gone.

21. Blend in what remains of the round-over with the pillowed face.

22. The finished faux tenons should protrude about 3/16".

23. Use 1/4" spacers to correctly position the rafter tails.

same seesaw motion with 220-grit. To blend in what remains of the round-over with the pillowed face use a flapping motion backed up with your thumb going through the same grits. Finish the end off with 320-grit.

Cut the faux tenon stock into lengths of about ½" and back bevel the leading edge as you would with an ebony plug. Spread a little glue around the inside perimeter of the hole and tap the faux tenon in with a plastic headed mallet. The finished faux tenons should protrude about ³⁄₁₆".

Finishing

Before finishing, perform a thorough inspection of the stands, looking for any scratches or dents. For a complete finishing schedule, refer to the discussion on page 111.

Attaching the Rafter Tail Assembly

With the finishing done, it's time to attach the rafter tail assembly to the leg/rail structure. First, make four small ¼" spacers to place between the legs and protruding rafter tail ends, as seen in photo. Using a caul to protect the finish, clamp the rafter tails in place.

Using an ¹¹⁄₆₄" taper bit with a counter bore, pre-drill for a #8 x 1 /3/4" flat head wood screw at the spot where the rafter tails pass over the rails. Be sure to drill the entire length of the screw to avoid splitting the rail. Cover the screws with a piece of ⅜" round felt. If the stands are to be placed on a hard surface, you might also want to place some felt pads on the bottom of the legs as well.

The speaker stands are now finished. Set them in place with your speakers on them. Put on some nice pleasing music, make yourself comfortable in your favorite chair, and enjoy!

24. Cover the screws.

25. The finished speaker stand. Photo by Richard McNamee.

Chapter 9

Seattle Mirror Frame

The Seattle Frame was originally conceived as a business sign. It framed my logo and did duty at my booth when I went to shows. Its potential as a part of my portfolio only occurred to me after it stole the show.

Given its long narrow shape, the design's obvious use would be as a mirror frame, either over a mantle or long sideboard. I had also entertained the idea of framing a sepia-toned archival city panorama of the Seattle skyline as seen from Elliot Bay. My search for a usable image has yet to yield something better than a waterfront panorama from the 1870s, which had been poorly "Photoshopped" (so to speak) at the time it was taken. I am still looking!

The design has definite elements of Greene & Greene, with the cloud-lifts and ebony pegs. But it also pays homage to Stickley, with the exposed tenons, and to Japanese influences with the tapered leg.

The Lower Rail Template

Before getting started, make a flexible guide-edge from a piece of 1" angle aluminum about 40 inches long. Cut a series of band saw kerfs about one-inch apart on one of the faces. Follow up by pre-drilling $\frac{5}{32}$" screw holes in every other kerfed finger.

The Seattle Mirror Frame.

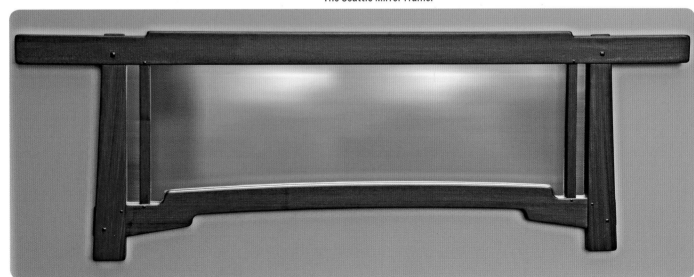

A. Lower Rail Template Layout

Layout for overall template shape.

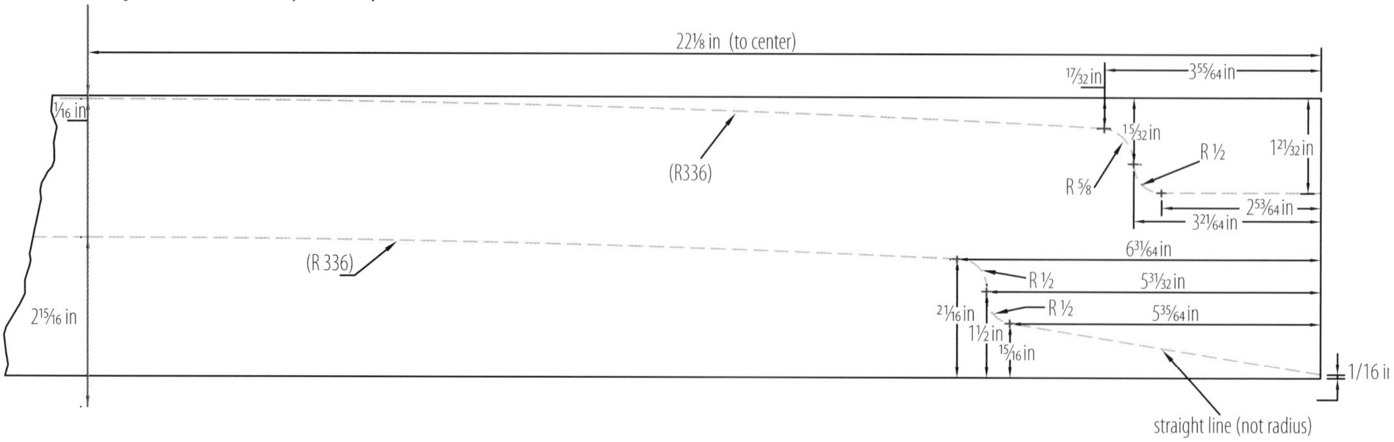

22⅛ in (to center)
17/32 in
3 55/64 in
1/16 in
15/32 in
R ½
1 21/32 in
(R336)
R ⅝
2 53/64 in
3 21/64 in
6 31/64 in
(R 336)
R ½
5 31/32 in
2 15/16 in
2 1/16 in
R ½
5 35/64 in
1½ in
15/16 in
1/16 in
straight line (not radius)

Cut a piece of MDF or Baltic birch to 4⅞" x 44¼. Referring to drawing A, lay out all the end points using a marking device capable of accuracy to within 1⁄64". An Incra marking rule is a good choice.

To create the two large arcs, bend the aluminum flexible guide-edge to connect the center and two end points. Strive for an evenly balanced arc. Temporarily secure with screws, then pencil in the resulting line. Use a rule to connect the end points of the short straight lines. Finish off the outline by using a Berol r-75 radius guide (or any object with a similar radius) to connect the cloud-lift end-points.

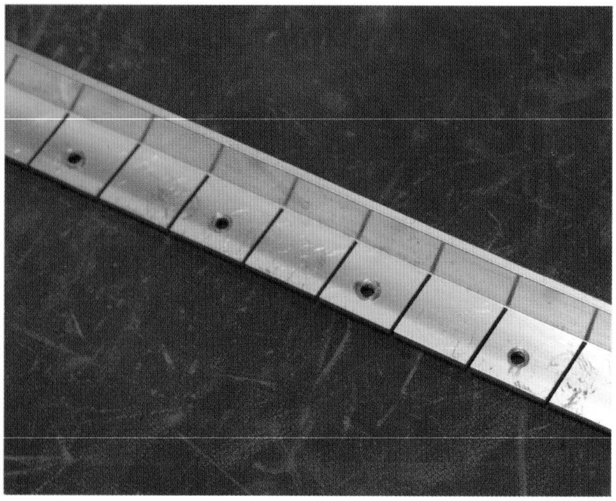

1. Angle aluminum with kerfs for laying out curves.

Cut List

Qty.	Description	Material	Thick	Wide	Long
1	Top Rail	Khaya	1⅛	3 3/16	63¾
2	"Legs"	Khaya	1	2 15/16	17 15/16
1	Bottom Rail	Khaya	⅞	4 ⅞	44¼
2	Auxiliary Posts	Khaya	⅜	1	13 17/32
2	Floating Tenon Stock	Any	⅜	2⅛	1½
2	Floating Tenon Stock	Any	⅜	1 11/16	1½
2	Faux Tenon	Khaya	⅜	2⅛	½
2	Faux Tenon	Khaya	⅜	1 11/16	½
1	12" Hangman Heavy Duty Mirror and Picture Frame Hanger available at Woodcraft				

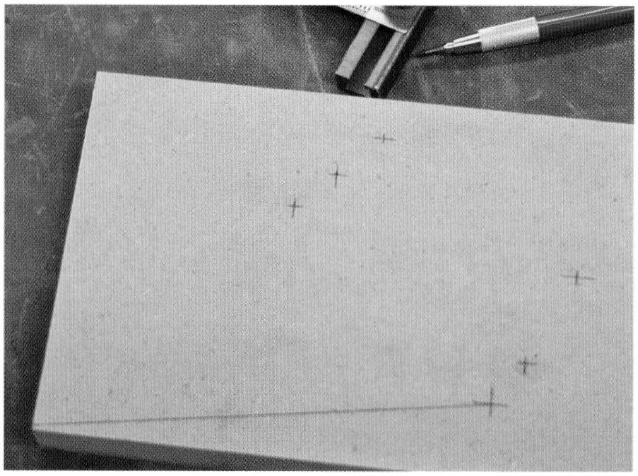

2. Lay out all the end points.

3. Use a radius guide to connect the end points

4. Route to the line with a flush trim bit and repeat for the other short straight lines.

5. Secure the aluminum flexible guide-edge to the large arcs and flush trim.

6. Use a spindle sander to sand to the line and fair-in to the connecting lines.

Once the layout is penciled in, the template can be cut to shape. Rough cut the entire outline to within approximately 1/16" of the line. Next, with a piece of scrap about 10" long, make a straight edge bearing guide. Line up the scrap-bearing guide to one of the short straight lines of the design and secure with screws. Route to the line with a flush trim bit and repeat for the other short straight lines. Be careful not to route into the cloud-lift when trimming the upper profile.

Now, line up the aluminum flexible guide-edge to one of the two large arcs and secure it with screws. On a router table with a top bearing flush trim bit, use the angled aluminum as a bearing guide and trim to the penciled line.

Repeat this procedure for the other large arc.

To form the cloud-lifts that connect the arch to the short horizontal lines, use a spindle sander to sand to the line and fair-in to the connecting lines. As a more consistent option, a master cloud-lift template can be utilized as described in my first book *Greene & Greene: Design Elements for the Workshop*.

The Top Rail Template

To make the template for the top rail, (drawing B) cut out a piece of scrap material measuring 3⅛" wide by 63¾" long. Set up the router table with a ½" straight bit. Split the fence so that the out-feed side is flush with the cutting edge of the bit. The in-feed side should be back of the out-feed side by exactly ⁷⁄₁₆". Going back to the scrap template stock, mark a line 11 ¹⁹⁄₃₂" down from both ends. Now run each end of the template stock through the router table setup, stopping at the drawn line.

7. The out-feed side is flush with the cutting edge of the bit.

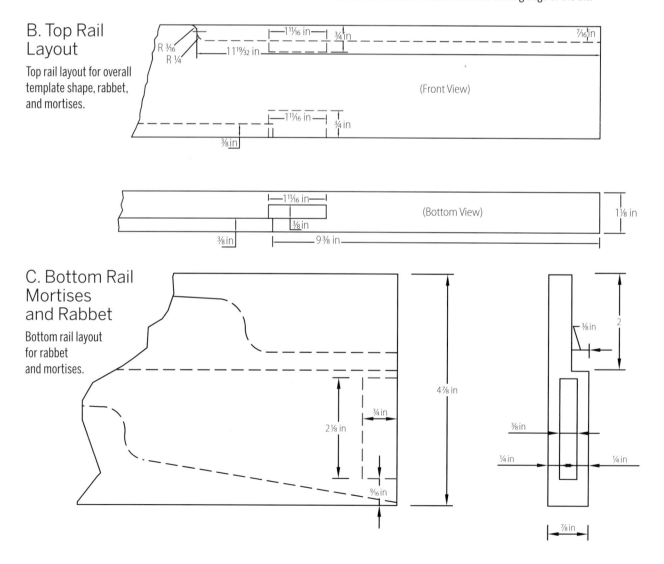

B. Top Rail Layout

Top rail layout for overall template shape, rabbet, and mortises.

C. Bottom Rail Mortises and Rabbet

Bottom rail layout for rabbet and mortises.

8. Run each end of the top rail template stock through the router table setup, stopping at the drawn line.

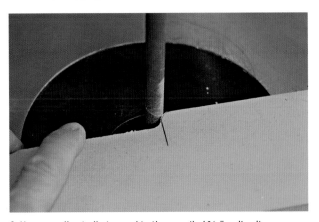

9. Use a small spindle to sand to the penciled ³⁄₁₆" radius line.

Draw in the adjoining ³⁄₁₆" radius to finish the cloud-lift's outline. Next, using a small (½" diameter or smaller) spindle sander setup, sand to the penciled ³⁄₁₆" radius line to complete the template.

Milling and Joinery

Set the templates aside and mill all the parts to their overall size. While the stock is still in rectangular form, now is the time to layout and cut the mortises (drawings B, C and D) for the floating tenon joinery. Use whatever mortising method you are most comfortable with. If you chose to employ traditional mortise and tenon joinery, add ¾" of length to the two legs and 1½" to the bottom rail to accommodate a ¾" tenon where the drawing calls for a mortise. Dominos are acceptable as well. At this time, do not machine the four stopped tee halving joints that join the auxiliary posts to the top and bottom rails. This will be done after assembly.

D. Leg Layout

Leg layout for overall shape, mortises and rabbet.

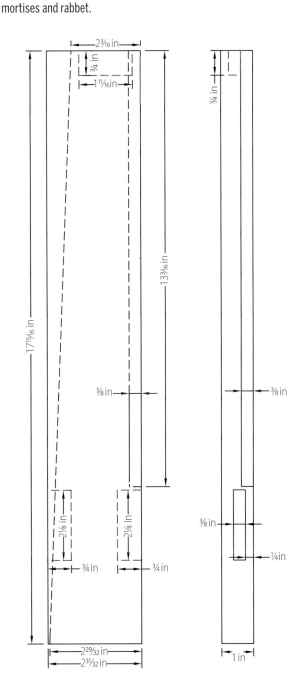

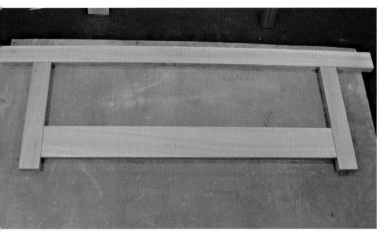

10. It is a good idea to dry fit all the pieces.

11. Adjust the height of the bit to exactly ⅜". Shown with support piece on out-feed side.

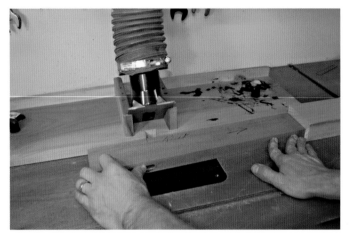

12. To rabbet the right leg, the stock needs to be in solid contact with the fence as it is slowly pivoted into the router bit.

13. Start the rabbet cut by placing the stock solidly against the end of the in-feed fence and slowly pivoting into the router bit.

With the major joinery complete, it is a good idea to mill out the floating tenons and dry fit all the pieces. If a problem arises, now is the time to fix it. Measure the distance between the bottom edge of the top rail and the top horizontal edge of the bottom rail. This measurement represents the shoulder length of the auxiliary posts, and if everything went as planned, that dimension should be 12 ²⁵⁄₃₂". Don't worry if it is not though; the shoulder length of the auxiliary posts can be adjusted later to match.

Rabbetting for the Mirror

The rabbet for the bottom rail (see drawing C) needs to be wider because of the arch. To begin, set up a router table with a ⅜" or larger straight bit. Adjust the height of the bit to exactly ⅜". Be sure to test all the setups on scrap material

first. Set the fence so that the bit's farthest cut (outside edge) is 2". Several passes will be needed to achieve the 2" of width needed. After the first pass, move the fence forward and make another pass. Repeat this process until the rabbet is complete. If you are not comfortable with router table setups, it may become necessary to position a support piece on the out-feed side of the fence for the last pass.

To route the left leg, place a block on the out-feed side of the fence to stop the cut 13³⁄₁₆" from the top of the leg (4¾" from the bottom end). For the right leg the stop will need to be placed on the in-feed side of the fence (see drawing D). Use caution with this setup. The stock needs to be in solid contact with the fence, near the stop block, as it is slowly pivoted into the router bit.

14. To shape the legs, first lay out the reverse taper in pencil. Next, band saw close to the line, then finish off with the edge sander.

15. Use a spindle sander to remove material from the cloud-lifts to avoid blowout.

16. Attach the template to the backsides of the stock and route flush.

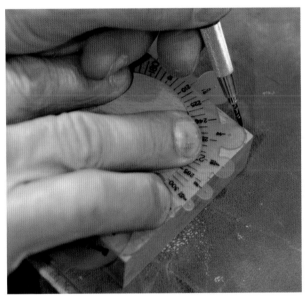

17. Mark out the ¼" radiuses.

The rabbet for the top rail (see drawing B) ends at 9⅜" from either end, but given the long length of the piece, the previous method using a stop block is not practical. On both sides of the router fence, calculate and mark the point where the ends of the stock will stop when the 9 ⅜" rabbet termination is reached. For safety, it is very important to start the cut by placing the stock solidly against the end of the in-feed fence and slowly pivoting into the router bit. If you are uncomfortable with the pivoting procedure to rabbet the legs and top rail, you can alternatively set up and use a hand held router with a rabbeting bit for this operation.

Shaping the Parts

To shape the legs, first layout the reverse taper in pencil (see drawing D). Next, band saw close to the line, then finish off with the edge sander. For the upper and lower rails trace the shape from the templates to the stock, then bandsaw close to the line.

Before routing, use a spindle sander to remove as much material from the cloud-lifts as possible to avoid blowout. Next, set up a bottom bearing flush trim bit in the router table. Attach the templates to the backsides of the stock with double back tape or screws, and route flush. With no "run-out" for the bearing, you must rest the stock against a solid object and pivot it into

18. Sanding to the ¼" radius lines at the ends of the legs.

19. If your method of making mortises produces round ends, now is the time to square the faux tenon holes.

20. Assemble the legs and rails after first sanding them to 220-grit.

the router bit. Again, if you are uncomfortable with the pivoting procedure, you can alternately clamp the parts to your bench and route flush with a hand held router, repositioning the clamps as necessary.

Finish off shaping by marking out the ¼" radiuses at the ends of the legs (see drawing D) and top rails (see drawing B). Waste most of the material away on the band saw and then sand to the line using an edge sander.

Next, set up a router with a ⅛" round-over bit and route all the face edges. If your method of making mortises produces round ends, now is the time to square the faux tenon holes. This can be done with a square hole punch or the hollow chisel from a mortiser.

Putting the Parts Together

The legs along with the top and bottom rails can now be sanded to 220-grit, then glued and clamped together. With the main body of the frame assembled, the corners of the backside rabbet can now be squared up with a chisel.

Next, verify the final distance between the top and bottom rails to be 12 ²⁵⁄₃₂". Check both sides, as it may not be the same. The joinery adds another ¾" to the overall length of the auxiliary posts, for a total dimension of 13 ¹⁷⁄₃₂". If your rail to rail measurement is not 12 ²⁵⁄₃₂", adjust the overall length to compensate and record the needed dimension for later use.

The auxiliary posts are attached to the frame by way of a stopped "T" halving joint. This joint will require a jig for a precisely positioned route out in the back side of the frame. As seen in drawing

21. The corners of the backside rabbet can now be squared up with a chisel.

22. Gluing up the jig for the stopped "T" halving joint.

E. Stopped "T" Halving Joint Jig

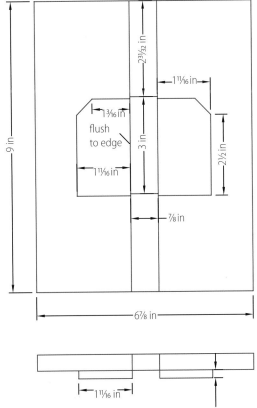

2³¹⁄₃₂ in

1¹¹⁄₁₆ in

1³⁄₁₆ in
flush
to edge

3 in

2½ in

1¹¹⁄₁₆ in

9 in

⅞ in

6⅞ in

⅝" collar ½" bit

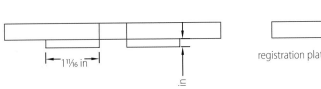

1¹¹⁄₁₆ in

in

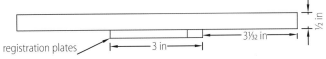

registration plates

3 in

3¹⁄₃₂ in

½ in

23. Before attaching the registration plates, bevel back about ½" of the material at one corner.

24. Set up a router with a ⅝" collar and a ½" up-cut spiral bit.

25. Square up the corners.

26. Run the faceside through first.

E, the jig is made from two pieces of ½" material, 3" wide and 9" long. These two pieces are joined by two more spacer pieces of ½" material that are ⅞" wide with a 3" gap between them. Before attaching the registration plates, bevel back about ½" of material at one corner. This will allow the plates to precisely register even if the rabbetted corners have not been squared up correctly.

Next, set up a router with a ⅝" collar and a ½" up-cut spiral bit. Set the depth so that the bit projects precisely ⅜" past the registration plates. Register the jig against the corner of the backside rabbeted edge (the beveled corner should be positioned into the corner) and route out the joint.

If everything went as planned, the jig should have produced a routed notch that starts flush with the back face of the rabbet and goes ¼" deep

and ¾" wide. The corners will be rounded and need to be squared up with a chisel.

The auxiliary posts can now be made. Only two are needed, but cut a couple of extra pieces about 15" (1½" over size) in length to use in joinery setup. First, set up a table saw with a zero-clearance throat plate and a supplementary wood fence clamped in place. With a rip blade (all flat bottom teeth), set the height to exactly ⅜". Now, move the fence up to, and just barely touching, the supplementary wood fence. The resulting cut should remove exactly ⅛" of material. Square up one end of one of the stock pieces, leaving it extra long. With a backup push block, run the face side through first to control blow out. Next, flip the piece 90 degrees to machine one edge, then 180 degrees to do the

27. The half lap tennon.

28. The auxiliary posts glued in place.

29. Sand until the pencil line is removed.

opposing edge. The resulting joint should be sort of a half lap tenon that measures ¼" thick by ⅜" long. Adjust the blade height and fence as needed. Keep in mind that you may have to make further adjustments if your routed cavity in the frame differs from what was intended. Once all adjustments are correct, go ahead and run the parts.

To finish off the frame assembly, put a ⅛" round-over on the long face edges of the auxiliary post, then sand them to 220-grit and glue them in place.

The Ebony Plugs

The frame has now taken on a definable form and appears to be nearly complete. But important details still await. The design requires 10 ebony plugs, 2 at ⅜", 6 at ³⁄₁₆", and 2 at ¼". The plugs sit proud of the surface and display a soft pillowed face. They imply an active role in the joinery, although they seldom play any actual part in construction. For details on ebony plugs, see Chapter 4.

The Faux Tenons

There are two sizes of exposed, faux tenons for this project: ⅜" x 2⅛" and ⅜" x 1¹¹⁄₁₆".

You should first verify that the openings you have match these sizes, and then, if necessary, adjust the sizes of the faux tenon stock accordingly. As with the ebony pegs, mill the stock out in long lengths. Next, using a router table, put a ⅛" round over on the end of the stock. With a pencil, mark a line down the center of the routed end. Starting with 150-grit and using a seesaw motion, sand until the pencil line is removed. Continue sanding using progressively higher grits until a grade of 320 is reached. Smooth out the transition points with your thumb backing the sandpaper in a sort of flapping motion. When complete, the rounded end should smoothly transit and show no discernible facets. Cut the finished tenon end off at about a ½-inch and bevel the insertion end. To insert the faux tenons,

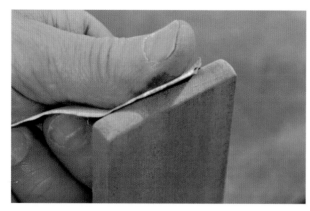

30. Smooth out the transition points.

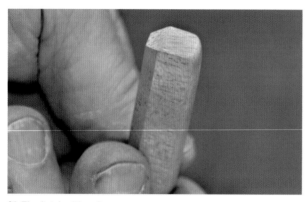

31. The finished faux tenon.

spread a little glue around the perimeter of the hole with a toothpick then gently tap them in place with a plastic headed mallet. The tenon ends should be about ³⁄₁₆" proud of the surface.

Making the Holes for the Ebony Plugs

Reference drawing F to layout the location for the ebony plugs. The holes are easy to produce using an appropriately sized square hole punch (available from Lee Valley Tools). To use the punch, center it on the pencil marks that represent the hole's location. Use a small square to insure proper alignment, and then tap on the tool just enough to register the points and make it stay put. With the tool still in place, use a regular twist bit that is ³⁄₆₄" under the size of the punch to drill out the hole to a depth of ³⁄₈". Do not use a brad point bit as it will cause damage to the bit. Now remove the drill and punch the tool to a depth of about ³⁄₈" with a steel hammer. Between hammer blows stop to wiggle the tool slightly,

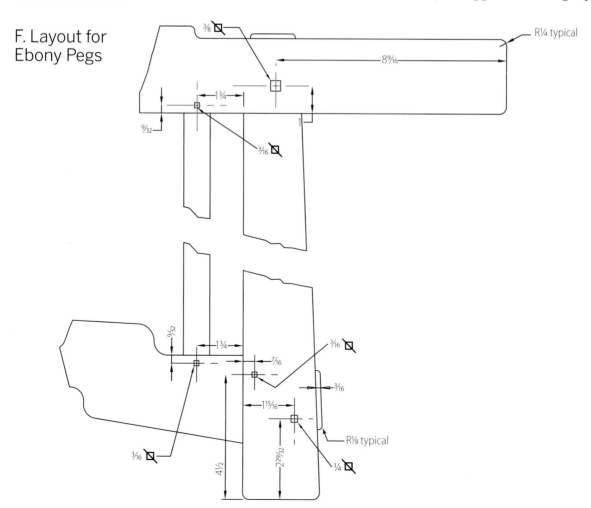

F. Layout for Ebony Pegs

32. Insert the faux tenons using a plastic headed mallet.

33. Use a small square to insure proper alignment.

34. Use a twist drill to drill out the hole.

35. Punch the tool to a depth of about ⅜" with a steel hammer.

36. Use a "back up" piece when punching the plug holes for the auxiliary posts.

37. Seating the plug.

this will aid in the removal. Additionally, treating the tool end with a lubricant such as Dri-Cote will further aid in easy removal.

Before removing the tool from the wood, re-insert the drill and drill to the same depth as before; this will remove the debris created by the punch. As the punch is pulled out, make an effort not to move it side to side, as this will enlarge the hole.

Machining the plug holes for the auxiliary posts will require a ⅜" "back up" piece to reduce the chance of blowing out the hole on the backside. Left over stock from the "faux tenon" stock should be just about the right thickness. Whatever back up piece is used it must take up the negative space left by the rabbet.

The hollow chisel from a mortising machine may also be used in a similar fashion to produce the holes, but its use for this purpose will damage it for use in a mortising machine.

Inserting the Plugs

Before setting in the plugs and tenon ends, take this chance to go over the piece one last time with 220-grit sandpaper. Hold the piece up to the light in a variety of directions in order to see any scratches or dents that need to be taken care of.

Inserting an ebony plug requires a little more care than the faux tenons. It is very easy to tap just a little too much and send the shoulder of the plug into the hole. Ideally the shoulder should stop just a few thousands shy of the hole. It is better to error on the side of leaving the plug just a bit too high. Use a plastic headed mallet to carefully seat the plug.

If you in fact have tapped the plug too far in, or for some other reason the plug needs to be removed, it is not difficult to do. First, use a center punch to establish a positive point starting point for a brad point bit. With a bit much smaller than the hole, drill out the center of the plug. Next, use a very small chisel to chip away from the drilled hole until a larger chisel can be used to finish it off.

The last bit of plug should just cleanly fall away from the walls of the hole, no matter how long the plug has been in place.

Finishing

An original finishing schedule relating to furniture from the Thorsen House (Greene & Greene 1908-10) calls for the use of Bichromate of Potash, also known as potassium dichromate. This is some nasty stuff and if a long life is part of your master plan, then this chemical reagent should be avoided. Potassium dichromate has been given a health hazard rating of "extreme" (causes cancer), a reactivity rating of "severe" (contact with oxidizable substances may cause extremely violent combustion), and a contact rating of "extreme" (pain and severe burn can occur).

Since long life is higher on my priority list than adherence to traditional methods, I have opted for an alternative finish.

The techniques and processes I use in furniture making evolve over time. Sometimes a better method is found and other times change is forced upon me. When I wrote my first book, *Greene & Greene: Design Elements for the Workshop*, I listed an aniline dye, English Brown Mahogany #43, for coloring the wood. Little was I to know that said aniline dye was about to be "no longer available." This precipitated numerous emails and phone calls from my readers asking for an alternative. What started out as misfortune turned into good fortune! I not only found an alternative, but an improved process as well.

Dye stains from General Finishes come in several colors and can be infinitely mixed to achieve the desired results. There is no pigment so it is actually a water based dye. I found that mixing 7 parts Orange Dye with 4 parts of Medium Brown Dye produces a beautiful brown with orange overtones. It is highly advisable to practice the entire finishing process on scrap material before committing it to your finished project.

To start the process, raise the grain with a wet rag. When dry, scuff sand with 600-grit. The idea here is not to sand too heavily. Wet the surface again. If the grain does not rise this time, you can

38. Using a stain applicator.

proceed to the dye application. If the grain rises, repeat the scuff sanding process until the grain does not rise.

While the General Finishes product will streak, it seems to be more user friendly in this regard than traditional aniline dyes. In order to mitigate any streaking or pooling that may occur, I like to apply three applications of the dye stain. Each succeeding coat will diminish undesirable elements left over from the previous coat. In between coats, minor touch-ups can be done with 600-grit sandpaper and a very light touch.

With a little practice, an even application can be achieved using a stain applicator such as a terry cloth covered sponge. Saturate the applicator with the dye and squeeze to apply. Wipe off any pooling and use compressed air to blow any excess out of the nooks and crannies.

For the top-coat, use General Finishes Arm-R-Seal satin. Be aware that improperly stored oily rags can spontaneously combust. Do not follow the instructions given on the label. Instead, apply the first liberal coat with a brush, then wait about ten minutes or until it starts to tack up, then wipe completely dry. Again, blow out any excess material from the nooks and crannies. The important thing here is to wipe the surface absolutely dry. When the first rag becomes saturated with finish, replace it with a new, unused, dry rag. Repeat this until the new rag remains dry and picks up no finish. This process takes a minimum of three coats and most often more, sometimes as many as seven or eight coats for a horizontal surface. With each additional coat the finish will set up a little faster. At some point it may become necessary to restrict the application to a smaller area in order to remove the finish before it sets up. If the finish does set up before it can be removed, simply apply more finish to loosen it up. In the end this will produce a satiny smooth finish. There is no need to sand between coats.

I normally do not apply a wax, but on the occasions when it is called for I prefer to use Renaissance Wax. Use this wax sparingly, not only because it is pricey, but also because not much is needed. Follow the instructions on the tin. Only do small areas at a time. If it dries and streaks before you can wipe it clean, use a little 0000-steel wool to correct it.

When the piece is finished, have a ¼" plate mirror installed, or if you have an appropriate image or art work to use, have ⅛" glass cut. To hang the mirror, use a 12" aluminum French cleat available at Woodcraft under the name "Hangman Heavy Duty Mirror and Picture Frame Hanger."

With the frame finished and hung in place, enjoy it, and hopefully in the very distant future pass it down to the next generation.

39. Keep the nooks and crannies clean.

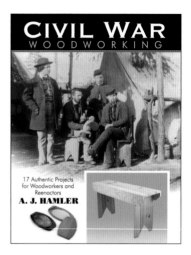
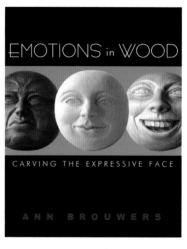
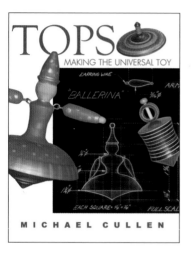
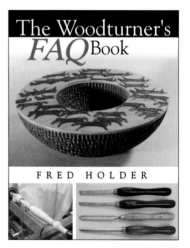

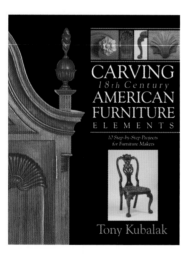